Measuring the Benefits of
Clean Air and Water

Measuring the Benefits of Clean Air and Water

Allen V. Kneese

RESOURCES FOR THE FUTURE, INC. / WASHINGTON, D.C.

Published by Resources for the Future, Inc.
1755 Massachusetts Avenue, N.W., Washington, D.C. 20036

Resources for the Future books are distributed worldwide by
The Johns Hopkins University Press.

Library of Congress Cataloging in Publication Data

Kneese, Allen V.
   Measuring the benefits of clean air and water.

   Bibliography: p.
   Includes index.
   1. Environmental policy—Cost effectiveness.
2. Environmental protection—Cost effectiveness.
3. Air—Pollution—Economic aspects. 4. Water—
Pollution—Economic aspects. I. Title.
HC79.E5K578   1984   338.4'33637392   84-17899
ISBN 0-915707-09-8 (pbk.)

RESOURCES FOR THE FUTURE INC.
1755 Massachusetts Avenue, N.W., Washington, D.C. 20036

Resources for the Future is a nonprofit organization for research and education in the development, conservation, and use of natural resources, including the quality of the environment. It was established in 1952 with the cooperation of the Ford Foundation. Grants for research are accepted from government and private sources only on the condition that RFF shall be solely responsible for the conduct of the research and free to make its results available to the public. Most of the work of Resources for the Future is carried out by its resident staff; part is supported by grants to universities and other nonprofit organizations. Unless otherwise stated, interpretations and conclusions in RFF publications are those of the authors; the organization takes responsibility for the selection of significant subjects for study, the competence of the researchers, and their freedom of inquiry.

This book is the product of RFF's Quality of the Environment Division, Clifford S. Russell, director. Allen V. Kneese is a senior fellow at Resources for the Future.

This book was edited by Jo Hinkel and designed by Elsa Williams. The figures were drawn by Arts and Words. The index was prepared by The Information Bank.

CONTENTS

PART III. CASE STUDIES IN RURAL AND REGIONAL AIR AND WATER POLLUTION

PART IV. CONCLUSION

PART V. BIBLIOGRAPHY AND INDEX

FOREWORD

It was not so very long ago that welfare economists dismissed physical externality problems as being limited to bucolic phenomena such as the relation between bee colonies and orchard pollination. And it remains true today that many scientists, policymakers, and interested citizens regard the application of economic principles to pollution problems—the arch example of physical externalities in the industrial world—as foolish, pointless, and even as evil.

Yet in the last twenty years, much has happened to make both these positions obsolete. On the one hand, pioneers—such as the author of this book—brought together threads from welfare economics with reasoning from the environmental sciences to create the new field of environmental economics. On the other, more and more citizens apparently have been persuaded that the pursuit of the perfectly clean and perfectly safe environment will involve either unacceptably high costs or unacceptably intrusive government regulation, or both.

Once it becomes politically possible to ask how clean and how safe, the tools of the economist become relevant to the debate. For a large subset of the body politic that moment of possibility was signaled in February 1981, when President Reagan issued his Executive Order 12291. This order requires the performance of benefit–cost analyses in connection with any major regulatory action, even if the governing legislation forbids the use of that analysis in the decision. Since that date there has been a flurry of research activity designed to make such analyses possible, for even today, the available tools are still relatively crude and untested.

However, the U.S. Environmental Protection Agency and the environmental economics profession were not caught entirely unprepared by the political arrival of benefit-cost analysis. Ever since its birth the discipline has been fascinated by the challenge of measuring the benefits of reducing harmful pollution effects, and a large literature attests to that fascination. And for the better part of a decade, the EPA—especially in the person of Alan Carlin—has encouraged and funded research on benefits estimation, an area not then in the forefront of environmental policy. This book describes the results of the EPA's program of methods development in language that will be accessible to a wide audience of interested citizens. One might say that the authors aim is to demystify benefits estimation with the idea that what we understand we are less likely to fear and resent.

As background it should be noted that this is not RFF's first foray into the benefits literature. Indeed, a complete catalog of our relevant efforts would be too long for this Foreword and would take us back to the very early days of the organization. It is worth mentioning, however, that RFF published a more technical volume in 1979, describing the then state of the art of benefit analysis (A. Myrick Freeman III, *The Benefits of Environmental Improvement*). Those readers of a technical bent may wish to treat this volume as an *hors d'oeuvre* to Freeman's *entrée*. But our intention is that many readers will find this book interesting and valuable in its own right.

Washington, D.C.
July 1984

Clifford S. Russell, Director
Quality of the Environment Division
Resources for the Future

ACKNOWLEDGMENTS

More than most, this book depends on the work of others. It is a nontechnical exposition of almost a decade of research, sponsored by the U.S. Environmental Protection Agency. To improve methods and data for estimating the benefits of air and water quality improvement or maintenance supplemental funds specifically for the writing and production of this book were provided by the EPA and the Andrew W. Mellon Foundation. The case studies reported in this book were performed by other members of the research team, although I had some hand in most of them. The technical reports on which I based the exposition of the cases are listed in the Bibliography, and the specific study (or studies) on which each chapter is based is acknowledged in an author's note to that chapter.

A special note of recognition goes to Alan Carlin, who was the EPA project officer for nearly all of the studies listed in the Bibliography. He should be recognized not only for his farsighted recognition of the need for methodological studies on environmental benefits estimation, but also because he managed to provide sustained funding for the enterprise. The latter is a feat only those who have dealt with the government in connection with funding of economic research will fully appreciate.

Finally, thanks are due to Jo Hinkel, who edited the book and assembled the list of Supplementary Readings; and to Martha A. Bari and Patricia A. Vasselo, who typed the manuscript.

Washington, D.C.
July 1984

Allen V. Kneese
Senior Fellow, Resources for
the Future

I

BASICS

Part I is a presentation of basic concepts and methods which underlie the case studies in Part II. Chapter 1 introduces benefit–cost analysis, the technique of policy analysis that, under Executive Order 12291, must be applied to all major federal regulatory actions. Chapter 2 explains the concept of economic benefits. Chapter 3 focuses on links, via natural systems, between actions that affect the environment and their effects on humans and why an understanding of those links is important for benefits estimation. Finally, chapter 4 discusses the problems of assigning economic values to those effects once they have been established.

1

INTRODUCTION TO BENEFIT–COST ANALYSIS

In the 1960s, the people of the United States became increasingly aware that the fruits of economic development were infected by the rot of environmental deterioration. Late in the decade and early in the 1970s, concern grew to such an extent that a number of laws were passed by the Congress aimed not only at stemming the deterioration of the environment, but improving its quality as well. As we move into the 1980s, environmental concerns—as attested by public opinion polls— remain vitally alive, but we face other major national difficulties as well. The economy is weak, productivity growth remains low, inflationary pressures still exist, and there appears to be no immediate hope for major improvement. In this adverse economic atmosphere, there is heightened interest as to whether the costly environmental regulations that have been put in place are, in fact, worthwhile. In trying to shed some light on this question, appeal is often made to an economic evaluation method called *benefit–cost analysis*.

Historic Development of Benefit–Cost Analysis

Benefit–cost analysis was developed initially to evaluate water resources investments by the federal water agencies, principally the U.S. Bureau of Reclamation and the U.S. Corps of Engineers. The general objective in this application was to provide a useful picture of the costs and gains associated with investments in water-development projects. The intellectual "father" of benefit–cost analysis was the nineteenth-century Frenchman, Jules Dupuit, who in 1844 wrote an often-cited study, "On the Measure of the Utility of Public Works." In this remarkable article, he recognized the concept of consumers' surplus (which is detailed in chapter 2) and saw that as a result the benefits of public works usually are not the same thing as the direct revenues that the public works projects will generate.

In the United States, the first contributions to the development of benefit–cost analysis did not come from the academic or research communities, but rather from government agencies. Almost from the nation's beginning, officials and agencies concerned with water resources development have been aware of the need for economic evaluation of public works projects. In 1808 Albert Gallatin, President Jefferson's secretary of the treasury, produced a report on transportation programs for the new nation in which he stressed the need for comparing the benefits with the costs of proposed water improvements. Early in this century the Federal Reclamation Act of 1902, which created the Bureau of Reclamation and was aimed at opening western lands to irrigation, required economic analysis of projects. The Flood Control Act of 1936 proposed a feasibility test for flood-control projects which requires that the benefits "to whomsoever they accrue" must exceed costs.

In 1946 the Federal Interagency River Basin Committee appointed a Subcommittee on Benefits and Costs to coordinate the practices of federal agencies in making benefit–cost analysis. In 1950 the subcommittee issued a landmark report entitled *Proposed Practices for Economic Analysis of River Basin Projects*. This document was fondly known by a generation of water-project analysts as the "Green Book." While never fully accepted either by its parent committee or the pertinent federal agencies, this report was remarkably sophisticated in its use of economic analysis and laid an intellectual foundation for research and debate in the water resources area, which made it unique among other major reports in the realm of public expenditures. It also provided general guidance for the routine development of benefit–cost analysis of water projects which persists until now, even though a successor report exists that is more adapted to the conditions of the present day.

Following the Green Book came some outstanding publications from the research and academic communities. Several volumes which appeared during the past twenty-five years have gone much further in clarifying the basic ideas underlying benefit–cost analysis and the methods for quantifying them. Eckstein's (1958) *Water Resource Development: The Economics of Project Evaluation* is particularly outstanding for its careful review and critique of federal agency practice with respect to benefit–cost analysis. *Water Supply: Economics Technology and Policy,* a clear exposition of principles together with applications to several important cases, was prepared by Hirschleifer, DeHaven, and Milliman (1960). A later study—*Design of Water Resource Systems*—especially notable for its deep probing into applications of systems analysis and computer technology within the framework of benefit–cost analysis, was produced by a group of economists, engineers, and hydrologists at Harvard (Maass and coauthors, 1962). The intervening years have seen considerable further work on the technique and a gradual expansion of it to areas outside the water resources field, some of them more or less natural extensions of the work on water resources. For example, the last two decades have seen many attempts to evaluate the benefits of outdoor recreation—both water-related and otherwise. A relatively recent book by Mishan (1976) looks at some applications other than water-related ones, but is in the mainstream of traditional benefit–cost analysis.

New Applications of Benefit–Cost Analysis

But the most striking development in recent years has been the application of benefit–cost analysis to the economic and environmental consequences of new technologies and scientific and regulatory programs. For example, the Atomic Energy Commission (before the Energy Resources and Development Administration and its successor, the Department of Energy, were created) used the technique to evaluate the fast breeder reactor program. The AEC published a report on this study in 1972. The technique has also been applied to other potential sources of environmental pollution and hazard. Two studies—one by the National Academy of Sciences (1974) and the other reported by Clement J. Jackson and coauthors (1976)—come to quite contrary conclusions regarding automotive emissions control. Other studies have been or are being conducted in the area of water quality-improvement policies, emissions control from stationary and mobile air-pollution sources, and the regulation of toxic substances.

Even while the technique was limited largely to the relatively straightforward problem of evaluating public works, economists frequently debated appropriate underlying concepts and methods of making quantitative estimates of benefits and costs—especially of benefits. Some of the discussion surrounded primarily technical issues, for example, ways of computing consumer surplus and how best to estimate demand functions for various outputs and equity issues (see chapter 2). Others were more clearly value and equity issues—for example, whether the distribution of benefits and costs among individuals or regions needed to be accounted for, or whether it was proper to consider only the sums over all affected parties.

Another central issue was to determine the proper weighting of benefits and costs occurring at different times. Known as the *discounting* issue, the term refers to the question of how to take into account the fact that normally the further into the future gains or losses accrue, the less heavily they are weighted by those who stand to do the gaining and losing, and therefore, by those who estimate them.

Application of benefit–cost analysis to issues such as nuclear radiation, the storage of atomic wastes, and the regulation of toxic substances in the various environmental media (both those substances which are immediately toxic to man and those which affect his life support or value systems) aggravate both the conceptual and quantification problems which exist in water-resource applications. There are several reasons for this.

First, while water-resource applications often involve the evaluation of public goods in the technical economic sense (see chapter 2), the bulk of outputs from such projects are electrical energy, irrigation water, navigation enhancement, flood control, and municipal and industrial water supplies. These outputs usually can be reasonably evaluated on the basis of some type of market price information because private developments often produce similar or closely related outputs. However, in the new applications, we are dealing entirely with situations in which useful information from existing markets is difficult, if not impossible, to establish.

Second, such matters as nuclear radiation and toxic materials relate to exposure of the whole population or large subpopulations to very subtle influences of which they may be entirely unaware. It is difficult to know what normative value individual preferences have under these circumstances, and clever methods of quantifying damages (that is, negative benefits) have to be evolved.

Third, the distributional issues involved in these applications concern not only monetary benefits and costs, but the distribution of actual physical hazard. For example, residents of an industrial city may suffer ill health resulting from pollution associated with the production of goods consumed in another locality. While it is possible that monetary equivalents to these risks could be developed, the ethical issues involved in such a situation go beyond the associated economic returns. This is especially true if compensation is not actually paid to damaged parties as in practice it usually is not.

Also, in some cases we are dealing with the after effects of a policy decision which could extend to hundreds of thousands of years and to many, many human generations. This raises the question of how the rights and preferences of future generations can be represented in the decision-making process. Realistically, the preferences of the existing generation must govern. Nonetheless, the question remains whether the simple direct desires of existing persons are to count exclusively, or whether justice demands that the present generation adopt some ethical rule (or rules) of a constitutional nature in considering problems which affect their descendants.

Thus the new applications of benefit–cost analysis bristle with ethical, value, and quantification issues. For the last several years a group of researchers located principally at Resources for the Future and the Universities of Wyoming and New Mexico have been working on research aimed at increasing our basic understanding and analysis of these issues. In the present book, a nontechnical summary of results from one of the most substantial thrusts of this research—methods development and quantitative estimation of benefits from air- and water-pollution control (that is, air- and water-quality maintenance or improvement) is presented. For the reader's convenience, a list of supplementary readings—including the volumes based on the aforementioned research—appears at the end of the book.

Before proceeding specifically to a discussion of the methods and results of the research, I think it will be useful to describe, in general terms, some of the basic ideas from the discipline of economics which were central to this research enterprise.

But before doing so, I wish to emphasize what this book is and what it is not. It is *not* an effort to provide a comprehensive review of environmental benefits studies in general. The case material in it comes from EPA-sponsored studies of air and water quality, conducted in a coordinated way over a number of years. And while this encompasses much of the research in the area, it is not an entirely comprehensive review.

Some boundary had to be set, and the one chosen seems reasonable on three grounds: (1) I have had some personal involvement in nearly all of the projects discussed and therefore feel more qualified to write about them than if I had only read about them; (2) these projects span the range of methodologies that have been developed for benefits-assessment work including bidding games, surveys, property value studies, wage differentials, risk-reduction evaluation, and mortality and morbidity cost estimation; and (3) they represent the results of a reasonably coherently planned program of research.

Accordingly, the book contains a relatively complete picture of the state of the art of benefits measurement for environmental improvements as of 1983. However, a further point should be made, and that is that these studies are deliberately at the frontier of the benefits-measurement craft. The reader should note especially that their chief intent was methodological improvement. Although quantitative estimates of benefits are given, they should be regarded as preliminary and experimental in character and, at best, an order-of-magnitude indication of the actual numbers. For this reason, I have not adjusted results for inflation, even though they are based on dollar amounts of the late seventies and early eighties. To refine them further would confer on them an unfounded aura of accuracy. Thus, it is within these bounds that the book proceeds.

References

Eckstein, Otto. 1958. *Water Resource Development: The Economics of Project Evaluation* (Cambridge, Mass., Harvard University Press).

Hirshleifer, Jack, James DeHaven, and Jerome W. Milliman. 1960. *Water Supply: Economics, Technology, and Policy* (Chicago, Ill., University of Chicago Press).

Jackson, Clement J., Calvin von Busek, Richard C. Schwing, and Bradford Southworth. 1976. "Benefit–Cost Analysis of Automotive Emissions Reductions," No. CMR 2265 (Warren, Mich., General Motors Corporation Research Laboratory).

Maass, Arthur, Maynard M. Hufschmidt, Robert Dorfman, Harold A. Thomas, Stephen A. Marglin, Jr., and Gordon Maskew Fair. 1962. *Design of Water-Resource Systems* (Cambridge, Mass., Harvard University Press).

Mishan, Ezra J. 1976. *Cost–Benefit Analysis: An Introduction* (New York, Praeger).

National Academy of Sciences, Coordinating Committee of Air Quality Studies. 1974. *The Costs and Benefits of Automobile Emission Control*, vol. 4 of *Air Quality and Automobile Emission Control*, series no. 19-24 (Washington, D.C.).

U.S. Atomic Energy Commission, Division of Reactor Development and Technology. 1972. *Updated (1970) Cost–Benefit Analysis of the U.S. Breeder Reactor Program*, No. 1184 (Washington, D.C., AEC).

U.S. Congress. Federal Interagency River Basin Committee. 1950. *Proposed Practices for Economic Analysis of River Basin Projects* (Washington, D.C., Government Printing Office).

2

WHAT ARE ECONOMIC BENEFITS?

While this book is intended to be a nontechnical presentation of our research on air- and water-quality benefits, some knowledge of a few key concepts from economic theory is essential to understanding both the research approaches taken and the results attained. The most central of these concepts is that of an economic demand for a *good*—that is, a material object which is valued by people—or for a *service*. When economists speak of demand, they are referring to the relationship between the real or hypothetical price of a good or service and the amount of it that consumers actually buy or would wish to buy per unit time at that price. Except in very unusual cases (one of which actually can be found in chapter 11) the amount consumers will want to take will be less, the higher the price. The discussion here of economic demand is simple and straightforward, but very compact.

It is important to keep one distinction clearly in mind when discussing economic demand: that is, the distinction between the demand of one individual or household—*individual demand*—and the "added up" demand of all individuals or households demanding that good or service—*aggregate demand*.[1] The latter is sought in doing benefit analysis but it is logically derived from the former.

[1]There is also the pertinent concept of derived demand. On the theory that "enough is too much," we will postpone discussion of this idea until we need it in connection with the case study presented in chapter 9.

Individual Demand

Let us start with a look at individual demand. Consider the following example of an individual's price–quantity relationship for the fictitious commodity, widgets, summarized below.

Price ($) of widgets	Quantity taken by consumer	Price ($) times quantity	Price ($) times incremental quantity	Accumulated price ($) times incremental quantity
8	0	0	0	0
7	1	7	7	7 (7)
6	2	12	6	13 (7 + 6)
5	3	15	5	18 (7 + 6 + 5)
4	4	16	4	22 (etc.)
3	5	15	3	25
2	6	12	2	27
1	7	7	1	28
0	8	0	0	28

At a price of $8, the consumer will buy no widgets, at $6, he will buy two, and so on. If, for whatever number he does buy, he is charged the same amount for each one (this is the usual practice in actually existing markets) then the third column, in which the price is multiplied by the number taken, will indicate how much he *actually* does pay. But if we could figure out a way to make him pay the maximum he is willing to pay for *each individual* unit (column four) or be deprived of having any widgets at all, then the accumulated price times incremental quantity shown in the last column would reflect his *total willingness to pay* for widgets. This is the amount he would pay in an all-or-nothing situation, where he either pays everything he would be willing to pay or he is deprived of widgets altogether.

Now suppose that our consumer decides he wishes to buy five widgets because the going price for widgets is $3 per item. He then actually pays $15, but if he had no alternative but to pay the maximum he *would have been willing to pay,* then he would have paid $25 for the five. The difference between what he did pay and what he would have been willing to pay—$10—may be thought to be some extra benefit which the consumer gets because there are such things as widgets available in the market. But because they are uniformly priced at a level less than his maximum willingness to pay, he gets this extra benefit. This additional value is called the *consumer's surplus* by economists. If it were to be the case that the consumer is not required to pay anything for the widgets, he takes eight and his consumer's surplus will be equal to his total willingness to pay—$28. In all cases where there is a positive price, his total willingness to pay will be greater than what he actually does pay because it will include what he actually does pay *and* his consumer's surplus. For example, if he buys four widgets, his willingness to pay equals what he actually does pay plus his consumer's surplus (that is, $16 + $6).

It is usual in expositions of consumer demand theory to express these ideas by plotting a *demand curve* for the individual. Figure 2-1 plots the numerical example just reviewed. In the simple example, the demand curve is a straight line. We generate this line by plotting a price–quantity pair point for each of the pairs shown in the numerical example, with interpolation between the points. It is apparent that the accumulated-price-times-incremental-quantity column (willingness to pay) is the accumulated area under the demand curve. To see this, observe that every individual-price-times-quantity pair makes a box on the graph, as is shown more abstractly in figure 2-2.

Since the curve represents every possible combination of such Ps and Qs (all possible boxes—imagine their width to be vanishingly small), it follows that the area under the whole curve is equal to the consumer's willingness to pay at zero price for Q.

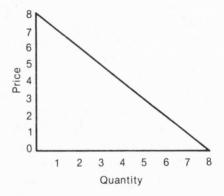

Figure 2-1.

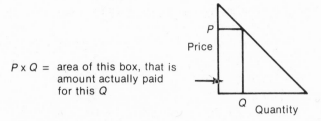

Figure 2-2.

Again, then, more abstractly than in the numerical example, let us review all the main ideas we have defined so far (figure 2-3).

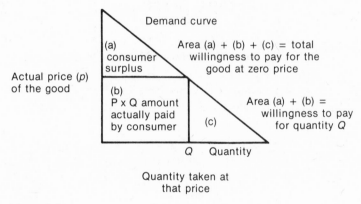

Figure 2-3.

Aggregate Demand

For many purposes (some of which will become clear later), we are interested in the total demand by all consumers for a good or service (in this case, widgets). How, then, do we add up the demands of all consumers in this market? If we are willing to make the assumption that all persons in the market for widgets should be treated equally, that is to say, everyone's demand counts the same in making up the sum, the answer is very easy—we just add up the quantities demanded at every price. For example, let us assume that there are two individuals in the widget market and both are exactly alike—let us say both are like the one depicted in the numerical example. In this case, the aggregate demand would be double the individual demand at any given price. For example, at the price of $5, aggregate Q would be 6, P × incremental $q = 2 \times 5 = 10$, P x q total $= 2 \times 15 = 30$, P x incremental q accumulated $= 2 \times 18 = 36$.

Again, this adding-up process is illustrated more abstractly and generally in figure 2-4.

There is no reason for individuals to be similar in order to make the adding up work. Everything is done in the same way if they are not, only the numbers are different. Once an aggregate demand curve has been calculated, the concepts of willingness to pay and consumer's surplus apply to it in the same way as to the individual demand curve (still assuming we are willing to treat everyone equally for this purpose).

Stated in its broadest terms, the objective of the research described in this book is to develop methods to derive estimates of the demand (willingness to pay) for cleaner air and water which would then be at least loosely comparable to demand estimates for other goods and services. This is to permit—at least roughly because of the uncertainties involved—comparison of the value that consumers place on cleaner air and water relative to other goods and services they buy. In practice, this is very difficult.

Unfortunately, even from the standpoint of ideas and concepts, we are not yet ready to proceed to quantitative economic analysis. In fact, cleaner air or water are not goods similar to widgets or to the many real goods and services—ranging from houses to pins—that can readily be bought and sold in markets. Economists refer to goods like widgets as *private goods,* and goods like cleaner environments as *public goods.*

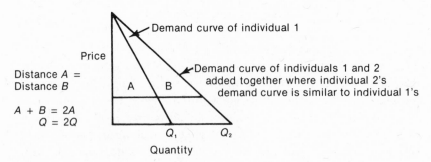

Figure 2-4.

Private Goods and Public Goods

In the economist's lexicon, widgets are private goods because they are divisible and separable. If you buy a widget and use it, that same widget does not at the same time render a service to me. If I buy and eat a banana, you cannot buy and eat that same banana. Such goods are easy for the private sector to produce and market because they come in distinct, divisible units and can be sold to distinct, divisible buyers. Should you, however, buy cleaner air, for example, in the city where you and I reside—say, by paying industries to clean up emissions—the services of that cleaner air are at the same time available to me, even though I did not pay anything for them. Such goods are called public goods because their units are not divisible and distinct. Their services are available to many persons at the same time, including those who do not pay for them, and unlike private goods the use of their services by one person does not diminish their availability to others. Private markets are very bad at producing such goods; indeed, there usually is no private economic incentive to produce them at all because while many people could benefit from them, no single individual usually has a sufficient incentive to pay for them.

Two chief implications for the research reported in this book flow from this situation. First, while in principle it is possible to think of an individual demand curve for cleaner air or water that is similar to that for widgets, there usually will not be market price information which will help *directly* in defining such a curve. Sometimes, as we will see, such information is helpful *indirectly*. This means further that development of methods for obtaining information on how consumers now value or would value cleaner air or water if they had more information is a very important and difficult task. To develop such methods was, as already stated, the chief objective of our research.

A second implication is that even if we have individual demand curves for public goods, we cannot properly add them up in the same way as for a private good.

To see this, refer to our widgets example on page 9. Instead of demand for widgets, assume that the columns refer to successively lower prices for air-quality improvements for an individual consumer and the quantities of improvement the consumer would want at those prices. Both $P \times Q$ and $P \times Q$ accumulated have the same interpretation as for private goods for this one individual. But now let us add a second

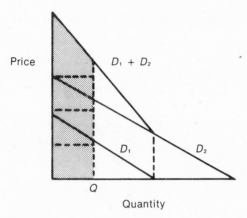

Figure 2-5.

consumer as we did in the private goods case. With the second consumer added in, it does not mean that more units of quantity of cleaner air will be taken at a given price, as was the case with the private good. The *same* units of quantity are available to both consumers. Thus, the willingness to pay for up to three units of cleaner air is $18 for the first individual *plus* $18 for those same three units, or a total of $36. The kind of summing done here is called *vertical* summing in contrast to the *horizontal* summing for private goods. It is easier to show the procedure when demand curves for the two individuals are not equal, so figure 2-5 assumes they are not. Individual demand curves are designated D_1 and D_2. For any given level of air quality, say Q, the willingness to pay for that level (the dotted area) is the willingness to pay of D_1 plus the willingness to pay of D_2 for the same quantity of air-quality improvement.

This total willingness to pay for Q units of clean air is, in economic terminology, the *benefit* of Q units of clean air. Since no price is charged for these Q units of air, it is also the consumer's surplus associated with the provision of Q units of clean air.

Compensation

A final note on concepts of demand; economic reasoning indicates that when we are considering a situation in which persons are deprived of something they otherwise would have had, as when previously clean air is polluted, willingness to pay for the clean air is not the fundamental test of its value to them. Rather, if they are to be as well off as before the change, one must ask how much they would have had to be *compensated* to be as well off as before. Generally speaking, *willingness to pay* is easier (although usually not easy) to estimate than required *compensation*. Economic theory indicates that the former will be equal to or smaller than the latter. In most of what follows, we will concentrate on willingness to pay as a conservative and usually more measurable quantity.

The aspiration in most of the quantitative studies reported here was to estimate willingness to pay, but we shall see that we must often be satisfied with results that resemble more the price-times-quantity value. But we do have the advantage of knowing in which direction the error lies in such an instance. We know from the earlier discussion that $P \times Q$ will never be larger than willingness to pay and that usually it will be smaller.

This completes the general discussion of economic benefits. More specific topics in the area will arise in connection with the case studies presented in Part II of this volume.

Chapter 3 treats briefly an essential element in the complete analysis of benefits from air- and water-quality improvement. This is the matter of establishing the link between a change in emissions of pollutants to the atmosphere or a watercourse on the one hand, and the ambient environmental conditions on the other, which, in some manner, adversely affect human beings.

There are two steps or links in the analysis of benefits from reducing emissions, the one just mentioned, and the other, once that link of emissions to human effect is established, what economic value is to be placed on that effect. The latter is the subject, in abstract terms, of chapter 4. The case studies presented in subsequent chapters concentrate primarily on quantifying the value to be placed on various pollution effects. But in chapter 3, as mentioned, I will discuss the links between emissions and their effects on humans. While this is not strictly an economic problem, the economist endeavoring to estimate benefits must often study these links as well because in many cases there is no usable preexisting information about them.

3

LINKS BETWEEN ACTIONS
AFFECTING THE ENVIRONMENT
AND THEIR EFFECTS ON HUMANS

As stated in chapter 2, an essential element in estimating the benefits from air- and water-pollution control is an understanding of how emissions control affects the environmental conditions which humans value. Such effects can be direct and easy to perceive, as when visibility is impaired, or indirect and difficult to perceive, as when air pollution produces chronic illness or when agricultural productivity is reduced by air contamination. This chapter briefly discusses the various links, and methods of estimating them, between emissions and ambient conditions that directly or indirectly affect humans. Understanding these connections is central to the discussions of economic evaluation which follow.

Health Links

Concern about health effects has been the basis for most of the air-pollution-control legislation in the United States. Links between emissions and health are subtle and difficult to establish, especially when one wishes to link *changes* in emissions to health states (as is necessary if we wish to estimate the demand for *improved air quality* or the demand for *air-quality maintenance*). One must determine the types of emissions, the concentration level of those emissions within the environment, the dose-response relationships (that is, how specific concentrations of an air pollutant are related to health), and the population at risk. The last three items are hard to estimate. Translations of emissions into concentrations in the environment (for example, converting the tons of sulfur oxide emitted into parts per million of sulfates at various points in the surrounding air) is best accomplished by means of special computer programs called *dispersion models*. These are imperfect at best, and usually it is not possible to verify them against observed conditions. The link between concentrations of substances in the environment and health effects is also hard to establish, especially if we are concerned with chronic rather than acute effects.

For example, there has been great concern about a possible link between air pollution and cancer. But cancer is a disease that usually appears many years after one has been exposed to carcinogenic substances—often some fifteen or twenty years later. Therefore, it is very difficult to sort out possible causes. Essentially, one can try to establish the link in two ways—by epidemiological studies and by animal studies with their subsequent extrapolation to human beings. The latter have well-known deficiencies, especially with respect to something as complex and subtle as air pollution, and in our research we made only limited use of them. Epidemiological studies observe conditions as they exist in the actual environment and—trying to control for other factors which also might be related to health—they endeavor to isolate the effect of pollution. The research team's effort to develop improved methods for quantifying the benefits of air-quality improvement involved several epidemiological experiments (see Part II for specific case studies). Needless to say, efforts to establish the link between air pollution and health are afflicted by great uncertainty.

Visual Quality

An emerging air-quality issue of central importance, especially in the western United States, is the impairment of visibility caused by air-quality deterioration. In this case, the link between emissions and their effects on humans is by direct perception of the degraded conditions. However, we are not only interested in how some fixed condition is perceived, but, in accordance with our discussion of economic demand in chapter 2, we wish to know what persons would be willing to pay for alternative, increasingly better, levels of air quality. Therefore, even though a person can perceive conditions directly, we must find ways of simulating situations other than those that exist at any given time.

While I reserve deeper discussion of how values can be attached to such conditions until chapter 4, it can be said here that the primary method is to ask carefully structured questions about how much people would be willing to pay for improved conditions. To solicit such information, simulated conditions are presented in visual form to the person being interviewed. Generally, this is done by means of photographs which have been taken during actual episodes of clean and dirty air that, at one time or another, have actually existed in the particular area being viewed.

A potential advancement over this procedure is computer simulation of changed conditions. In this technology, a slide of a particular scene is put in digital (numerical) form so that it can be replicated by a computer on a high-resolution television screen. Then computations are made about the effect that a hypothetical change in emissions—associated, say, with a projected new power plant at some specified distance and direction from the scene—would have on visibility. Since this calculation is also numerical, the computer then can simulate in pictorial form, on the television screen, the changed conditions of visibility. Development of this latter technique has been part of the projects reported here, but because of the then existing state of the art our efforts to obtain consumer values for visibility had to be based on actual pictures.

Agricultural Productivity Links

Agriculture may be adversely affected by air pollution. Plants may suffer from acid rain resulting from emissions of sulfur or nitrogen compounds, or may be weakened and made more subject to disease by their exposure to ozone. Since vegetation may be influenced by many factors, only one of which is pollution, isolating this effect is not so straightforward as it first might appear. However, that such damage does exist is well documented. Associations between monitored levels of air pollution and crop production are reasonably well established, especially in southern California (see chapter 9). But, as in the case of visual impacts and health, we are interested not only in what effect existing levels of pollution have on production, but also in what impact changes in pollution levels would have. Again, this means that, at least in principle, estimates of real or hypothetical emissions changes must be translated into ambient conditions with dispersion models, crops that may be especially sensitive must be identified, and exposed acreage calculated. Estimating the effects on consumer welfare via their derived demand (explained in chapter 9) for cleaner air for agriculture presents a particularly subtle and difficult problem. But that is a subject for chapter 4.

Links in Watercourses

I have repeatedly emphasized the need for establishing a link between pollution discharge and effects on humans or things in the environment that humans value. Unfortunately, the needed dispersion models for air quality are not available in all places—no nationwide model is available, nor, for that matter, is one feasible given the present state of the art. Accordingly, various simplifications often must be made in studying air-quality benefits—especially ones that are aimed at estimating national benefits. These short cuts will be described in connection with the cases as the need arises. Fortunately, we are in somewhat better shape for water quality where impacts of changes in wastewater effluent discharges on the aquatic environment must similarly be forecast. Resources for the Future has built and is steadily improving a National Water Quality Network Model (Gianessi and coauthors, 1981). This model simulates, by means of a computer, water-quality changes associated with changes in effluent discharges in the main watercourses of the nation, as shown in figure 3-1.

The network of water bodies contains 304 rivers, 175 lakes and reservoirs, 37 bays, 10 segments of Great Lakes shorelines—about 40 percent of the nation's freshwater surface area overall—and 26 ocean shoreline segments. Pollutants can be injected into the system at particular points (municipal and industrial discharges) and uniformly between them (polluted runoff from the countryside). The computer model then simulates the transport, degradation, and transformation processes that occur in the water body and calculates a number of water-quality characteristics at any point in the system, taking account of all of the points of discharge that affect that location. This capability, when translated further into areas of water rendered suitable for various recreational activities by pollution-control policies, proved very useful in the benefits from

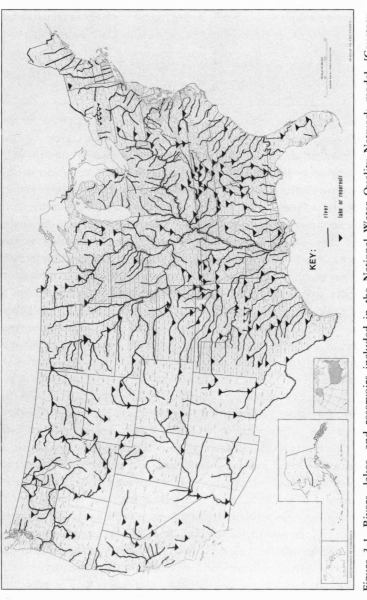

Figure 3-1. Rivers, lakes, and reservoirs included in the National Water Quality Network model. [Courtesy, Leonard P. Gianessi, Henry M. Peskin, and G. K. Young, "Analysis of National Water Pollution Control Policies: 1. A National Network Model," *Water Resources Research* vol. 17, no. 4 (August 1981) p. 797. Copyright © American Geophysical Union.]

recreational fishing project (see chapter 10). Unfortunately, at this time the model can handle only a few of the more conventional, better understood types of pollution—biochemical oxygen demand resulting from bacterial degradation of organic matter and suspended sediment, for example. Subtler influences on water quality presently elude it, such as the effects on aquatic ecosystems of the introduction of acid from environmental sources, both because the necessary data are not available and because the mechanisms for instream transformation have not been sufficiently understood and are not reflected in working models.

Aquatic Ecosystem Effects

Over time, it has become increasingly apparent that rainout and other types of deposition of materials from the atmosphere are major sources of contamination of watercourses, and as a result interest has been focused on acid deposition. When fossil fuels—especially coal—are burned, compounds of sulfur and nitrogen are released along with the other flue gases. Automobiles are also an important source of nitrogen emissions. Through chemical transformation processes in the atmosphere, these substances are partly converted to sulfuric and nitric acid. When this acid rains out of the atmosphere or is otherwise deposited in watercourses, especially lakes, they may become so acid that they cannot continue to support fish life. Also, increasingly acid soils can affect plant life adversely. Understanding the link between emissions at particular sources and such ecological effects is difficult, and research on that question is in its infancy. In principle, we need to understand quantitatively the processes of dispersion in the atmosphere (in this case, for very long distances—possibly thousands of miles), deposition processes, effects on acidity of the stream and related phenomena (for example, increased acidity may cause toxic metals to dissolve), and finally, the ways in which aquatic life is affected by the acidity. In practice (see chapter 11) we must make do with much less knowledge than this in our quest for the benefits of controlling acids from the atmosphere. Moreover, what we do know about the links between increasing acidity and fish life suggests that it is quite complex. For instance, it seems that as a certain critical level of acid in the water body is reached, damage to aquatic life mounts drastically with small further increases, but that damage then increases much more slowly, if at all, with further increases. Also, once damage has occurred, it may not be reversible by any practically available technology. Both these characteristics have substantial implications for the economic evaluation of benefits from controlling acidity in water bodies (see chapter 11).

Materials Damage

As well as having adverse aquatic ecosystem effects, the deposition of acid or its precursors is the major cause of materials damage from air pollution. Again, dispersion and deposition processes must be understood, but the actual damaging effects are chemical rather than biological in nature. For example, sulfuric acid reacts with the carbonate in limestone and destroys the stone. In addition, acids etch metals and cause corrosion. Similarly, fabrics and plastics can be damaged. Unfortunately, quantitative understanding and predictability of these phenomena is extremely primitive so that, once again, strong assumptions must be employed if damages, especially damages associated with changed conditions, are to be estimated.

Groundwater Links

One of the links most difficult to simulate is that between pollution discharge and groundwater. This is so because (1) far fewer resources have gone into increasing our knowledge of groundwater than have been devoted to surface waters and to air; (2) groundwater flow is often highly complicated; and (3) it is very difficult and expensive to make accurate measurements (holes must be bored to different depths through varying strata). Because it is a highly specialized area and because establishing the necessary links has been such an integral part of the benefits study of controlling groundwater contamination, further discussion will be deferred until chapter 11.

The discussion in this chapter, unfortunately, illustrates that our understanding of exactly how natural systems are affected by man's discharge of pollutants is still very limited. The uncertainties of knowledge about these connections are fully as great as the uncertainties about how to do the actual economic evaluations. Thus we are studying, in the experiments reported in this volume, something more akin to a craft than an exact science.

Chapter 4 discusses in very general terms some methodological aspects of placing an economic value on air- and water-pollution effects on the environment once they are identified and quantitatively estimated. Each of the methods discussed is employed and further explained in one or more of the case studies found in Part II.

Reference

Gianessi, Leonard P., Henry M. Peskin, and G. K. Young. 1981. "Analysis of National Water Pollution Control Policies: 1. A National Network Model," *Water Resources Research* vol. 17, no. 4 (August) pp. 796–801.

4

ASSIGNING ECONOMIC VALUES TO CLEANER AIR AND WATER

Once links have been established between humanly controllable actions that affect the environment and their associated direct and indirect effects on humans, then the central problem addressed by the research reported here arises—how to measure the economic demand for cleaner air and water. That is to say, what is the economic value to be attached to a given level, or successively higher levels, of improvements to air or water quality or to protecting the existing level of quality from deterioration? The method for estimating these values necessarily differs among the various effects associated with the deterioration of air and water quality. This is partly in response to a specific situation—for example, whether it affects consumers directly or indirectly—and partly a matter of the types of data it is practical to acquire. As further background for the case studies in Part II, I briefly will review some central issues in the economic evaluation of cleaner air and water.

Valuing Health Risks

The studies of health effects reported in chapters 5 and 6 focus on the possibility that air pollution may cause chronic disease, which in turn may contribute to higher death rates (mortality) or nonfatal sickness (morbidity). One central concern, if one is to calculate a benefit in monetary terms, is what value to place on reduced mortality. How much would people be willing to pay for a reduction in their risk of earlier death, or how much would they have to be compensated to voluntarily accept an increase in this risk?

Economists in the past have attempted to value human life as the future earnings over an individual's lifetime.[1] This approach, however, is no longer viewed as acceptable. In the first place, it assumes that the value of life can, in fact, be measured in economic terms—a point certainly open to debate. Second, it implies that the lives of children, housewives, retired, or other unemployed individuals are worth less than the lives of employed heads of households. Nearly everyone would find these implications ethically unacceptable.

Nearly twenty years ago, the American economist Thomas C. Shelling was the first to distinguish between the concept of the cost of statistical risk and efforts to value human life based on lost earnings. The cost-of-risk idea is ethically more appealing than attempts to value a particular human life. The effort here is to put a value on a small increase or decrease in the probability of death for anonymous, statistical persons. Implementation of this approach usually has involved a search for information about how much people have to be compensated to voluntarily accept a small increase in risk in occupations differing in riskiness—say, the risk of additional death per 1,000 persons. Thaler and Rosen (1975), using wage differences between jobs varying in the level of job-associated risk of death, were apparently the first to estimate explicitly the value of changes in safety. They observed that workers in high-risk jobs receive higher wages, and a value of safety can be imputed by examining these risk-related wage differences. Other factors that influence wages were statistically held constant by use of a technique called regression analysis (this method is briefly explained in chapter 5). Unfortunately, however, the Thaler and Rosen study deals with a class of individuals who, because they are engaged in risky occupations, may be more willing to accept risk than the rest of the population. Even so, the estimate Thaler and Rosen make suggests that a small reduction in risk over a large number of individuals which saves one life is worth about $340,000 (in mid-

---

[1] For those familiar with the concept of present value, it should be explained that the value used is actually the discounted present value of expected future earnings.

1970s dollars). This is far higher than the numbers obtained in lost-earnings studies.

Another study by Blomquist (1979), which examines seat belt use, suggests that the figure for a lost life might be $260,000. This study first estimates how people value their own time and then imputes a value of safety from the amount of time a sample of individuals spent in buckling seat belts. It may be noted that unlike the Thaler and Rosen result, this is a "willingness-to-pay" rather than a "compensation" measure. The result may, however, also be biased downward because individuals seem to perceive risks differently when an element of personal control, such as driving an automobile, exists rather than when an involuntary, individually uncontrollable risk is at issue, as is the case with environmental risk.

Finally, Smith (1974), in a study similar to Thaler's and Rosen's, but for a more typical population, found that the needed compensation to save one life may exceed $1 million. Numbers even higher than this have been reported in the literature.

Clearly, the cost of risk is not precisely known, and perhaps will never be, since attitudes—in particular, risk-averseness—presumably can change over time, between groups, and even can vary in different situations. But, we at least have a range of values with which to make order-of-magnitude estimates of the costs of environmental risks. Likely values lie between $250,000 and $1 million per life, valued in mid-1970s dollars.

There are some additional points to be made about valuing mortality risk by a particular number derived from observed behavior of people concerning risk. First, no distinction is made with respect to age, sex, employment, or other personal variables. To paraphrase Gertrude Stein, "a life is a life is a life." This seems ethically acceptable, but well might be the subject for debate. Second, this analysis does not give attention to the pain and suffering associated with different causes of mortality or to the cost of nonfatal diseases (morbidity). Third, the value obtained from existing studies does not vary with the degree of risk. To put the matter in terms of economic demand, this means that the demand curve for mortality reduction vis-à-vis pollution looks like that depicted in figure 4-1.

While, as stated in chapter 2, one generally expects price to decline as quantity increases, this constant value may be defensible within the present context because in the case of air pollution we are speaking about

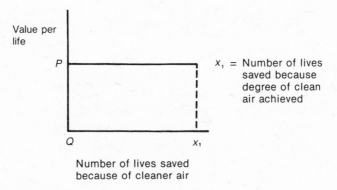

Figure 4-1.

small changes in the general risk to health. Over such a small range, it is not unreasonable to think that the value of risk reduction would remain about constant.

Morbidity

Pollutants can, of course, do great harm to health without actually killing. A number of studies have tried to evaluate the extent of this harm by first estimating the number of days lost from work because of pollution, and then, obtaining an economic value by multiplying the number of lost workdays by the average wage rate. This procedure is incomplete for several reasons: it does not value the cost of sickness for persons who are not in the labor force, that is, it neglects the disutility of the sickness itself. Also, it does not recognize that people can protect themselves to some extent, and at some cost against sickness (say, by installing an air filter). Approaches that recognize and account for these factors are sorely needed.

Visual Perception

As noted in chapter 3, questions about the value of visibility impacts have become highly significant in air-quality policy, especially as it applies to conditions in the mountainous West, where unusually clean air and the associated large, bright landscapes are highly prized by many people. The question of how to value such effects is a very difficult one. In an urban area, one might consider using differences in housing property values as an indication of the aesthetic values people attach to air clarity, and this approach will be discussed later. But in vast, scenic rural areas such as national parks, this clearly is not feasible. Thus, it becomes necessary to develop and use alternative methods.

The method chosen for our research used questions posed to recreationists and others affected by visibility impacts in an effort to discover their preferences and values. In all cases studied, the respondent was confronted with an image of possible changes in air quality at a particular site, in the form of carefully prepared photographs, and asked to state a value for it. The respondent was also asked to reveal other pertinent personal characteristics. This approach is referred to in the trade as a *bidding game.* Respondents can be queried as to their willingness to pay for the cleaner air conditions, the minimum compensation necessary for them to accept a change, what potential site or activity could substitute for the one in question, and their income, age, sex, and other factors. As the case studies in Part II show, responses to these questions can be used to estimate demand curves for cleaner air.

The major concern in using bidding games or other survey questionnaire techniques (such as the one used for water quality in chapter 10) to construct demand curves is that the reply to questions may be biased, either because the interviewee wishes to deceive or because of problems in the way questions are posed. Possible biases which could well exist in theory have been a major preoccupation of researchers pursuing the bidding game and other survey approaches.

The major types of bias identified in our work are (1) *strategic bias,* which means that the respondent may attempt to influence the outcome or result by not responding truthfully; (2) *information bias,* which results from lack of complete information on the part of the respondent; (3) *starting-point bias,* where the respondent may be influenced by the opening bid which is usually suggested by the interviewer; and (4) *hypothetical bias,* which could result from the inability to confront the respondent with an actual situation, for example, using a photograph rather than an actual scene.

The bidding game and other survey techniques are sufficiently central to the research in several of the case studies, and possible biases in results are sufficiently important to merit special attention.

Strategic Bias

Most economists have long supposed that direct revelation of consumer preferences for public goods (defined in chapter 2) would be impossible. In particular, the so-called free-rider problem would arise because the public goods situation gives individuals incentives to misstate their preferences. For example, if nearby residents were asked how much they were willing to pay to clean up the air near a coal-fired power plant, and if they suspected that control costs would be borne by consumers and owners elsewhere, local residents might well have an incentive to greatly overstate their actual willingness to pay since, in fact, they would not have to pay anything. On the other hand, if residents believed that they would be taxed an amount equal to their own individual willingness to pay, then a clear incentive would exist to understate their own true value, since their individual bid would have a negligible effect on the outcome in any case.

It is thus apparent that different techniques aimed at eliciting willingness to pay may generate their own variety of biases. For example, if respondents are told that the average of their bids to prevent construction of a power plant near a national park will be used to set an entrance fee to the park, those individuals who suspect their willingness to pay to be greater than the average willingness to pay will have an incentive to overstate their bid. They, in fact, in principle have an incentive to try to raise the average bid as close as possible to their own true willingness to pay. In other words, individuals will—again, in principle—have incentives to misstate their own preferences in an attempt to impose their preferences on others.

Information Bias

Since bidding games are hypothetical, answers obtained by this technique will not be based on information or perceptions as complete as those that applied if consumers based their answers on real experiences. Typically, consumers do reevaluate actual decisions on the basis of experience. Thus, a recreationist might respond to a hypothetical decrease in air quality at one location with a low bid, thinking that other nearby sites would make good substitutes. However, in a real situation, the recreationist might find that other sites involve more travel costs and are less satisfactory than imagined. Clearly, then, the information presented to the respondent in a questionnaire relating to substitution possibilities and alternative costs may well bias the stated willingness to pay. On the other hand, there may be no amount of verbally conveyed or written information that can fully substitute for the actual experience.

Starting-Point Bias

Central to the bidding-game approach are questions on willingness to pay (or compensation, or both) for hypothetical changes in environmental quality. It may be that it is better to ask the interviewee a question with a yes or no answer rather than a question requiring independent quantitative estimation on his or her part. Assuming that yes–no responses are desirable, it becomes necessary to suggest a starting bid or minimal level of compensation. Here the potential bias arises because the interviewee's final reply may be influenced by the opening bid. This possible bias comes from at least two possible sources. First, the bid itself may suggest to the respondent the approximate range of appropriate bids. Accordingly, he or she may respond differently, depending on the amount of the starting bid. Second, if the respondent values time highly, he or she may become "bored" or irritated with going through a lengthy bidding process. In consequence, if the suggested starting bid is substantially different from his actual willingness to pay, the bidding process may yield inaccurate results. The effect of these two types of starting-point biases may substantially influence the accuracy of bidding-game valuation and, therefore, the usefulness of this approach for assessment of preferences with respect to air pollution.

Hypothetical Bias

The bidding game requires suggesting, by way of pictures, a change in air quality so that it is believable to the respondent and accurately depicts a potential change. In addition, the change must be fully understandable to the respondent, that is, he or she must be able to understand most, if not all, of its ramifications. Finally, the respondent must believe that the change might occur and that his or her bid might have an effect on both the possibility and magnitude of change in air quality. If these conditions are not fulfilled, the hypothetical nature of bidding approaches will make their application to air-quality issues dubious and may bias the respondent's answers up or down. However, unlike other types of biases, it is extremely difficult to measure the extent of hypothetical bias since it depends not only on how well structured the interview is, but also on uncontrollable factors such as attitudes, the interviewer's style of presentation, the recreationist's "mood," and other factors.

Conclusions About Bidding-Game Biases

To test for the presence and importance of bias and to assist in developing methods in controlling for it, several of the projects reported below ran experiments using bidding games and surveys. The experiments show that all forms of bias can definitely exist. But it appears that problems of strategic, information, or starting-point bias are all surmountable with proper questionnaire design and statistical analysis. This—plus the comparison with an alternative valuation method discussed in chapter 7, and a technique developed in the National Water Quality Survey reported in chapter 10—suggests that well-designed survey techniques can produce reasonably reliable information about the value of air and water quality and other public goods.

Valuing Water-Based Recreation

Much work has been done by economists on the problem of evaluating water-based recreation and aesthetic values, and many methods have been applied to the problem. These include bidding games, other types of surveys, inferences from the value of waterfront properties, and a method based on travel costs to particular sites. In the two studies reported in chapter 10, a survey method was used in one and the travel-cost method in the other. For present purposes we distinguish between bidding games and surveys (see the previous section), even though they both ask respondents questions about their willingness to pay. All the bidding games reported in this volume pertain to the evaluation of quality changes at particular sites, and the sample population may or may not be, but usually is not, randomly selected from the general population. For example, if the technique involves interviews at the site, the sample population consists of those who happen to be at the site during the interviewing, and there is no reason to believe that those questioned actually are a random representation of the population at large. Surveys, as the term is used here, always choose their respondents randomly from the national population. This is an important feature for the study reported in chapter 10 because it was explicitly designed to provide national benefit estimates, and randomness permits an extrapolation of the sample results to the whole population by statistically acceptable procedures. In addition, this study endeavors to measure benefits of water-quality improvement that may accrue to people even though they may not be direct users of these water bodies. These benefits are variously called nonuser, intrinsic, or existence benefits.

The other benefits study reported in chapter 10 also had as its objective benefits estimation on a national level, but was "site-specific" (if site is interpreted to be a large geographic area) and focused only on actual or potential users of water bodies for recreational purposes, specifically, sport fishing. It employed, as one element, the travel-cost method to evaluate benefits to recreational fishing. This method was developed at RFF many years ago and is a well-established technique of recreational benefits evaluation that has been been used many times by economists, planners, and others to evaluate specific recreation sites. The novelty of the study reported in chapter 10 is its ingenious application of the methods to the particular problem of obtaining a *national* benefit estimate for recreational fishing associated with water-quality improvement.

Actual applications of the travel-cost technique are often quite complicated. Here I wish only to convey to the reader the general concept of how the method is used to construct a demand curve for a recreation site. The basic idea is that increased access cost that is associated with user distance from a desirable recreation site will tend to affect recreation visits in the same manner as an increase in access cost resulting from a hypothetical rise in an admission fee. If it were feasible to experiment with the fee, hypothetically setting it from zero to increasingly higher levels, it would, of course, be possible to define a relationship between demand and price (a demand function, as discussed in chapter 2). The basic principle of the procedure can be clarified by a simple numerical example.

Assume that we have divided the "market area" for a recreation site into four zones at different distances from it, and we have the information shown in table 4-1 about each zone.

If there is no entrance fee, there will be 1,200 visitors (say, per year) and that gives us one point on the demand curve, that for a zero price.

Table 4-1. The Relationship Between Site Visit and Travel Distance

Zone	Population	Access (travel) cost ($) to site	No. of visitors	Visits per 1,000 population
1	1,000	1	500	500
2	2,000	2	400	200
3	3,000	3	300	100
4	4,000	4	0	0
			1,200[a]	

[a] Total visits at zero entrance fee.

This is shown in figure 4-2. Now let us assume that an entrance fee of $1.00 per visit is levied. This is taken to have the same effect on visitation rates as a $1.00 difference in access cost related to distance. Accordingly, the visitation rate in Zone 1 will drop to that of Zone 2 which has a $1.00 higher access cost. Therefore, instead of a visitation rate of 500 persons per 1,000 persons from Zone 1, the rate will drop to 200. Since there are 1,000 persons in Zone 1, this means that there will be a total of 200 visitors from there. Zone 2's visitation rate will drop to that of Zone 3, which has a $1.00 higher access cost than Zone 2, that is, it will drop to 100 visits per 1,000 population. Since Zone 2 has 2,000 inhabitants, this means a total of 200 visitors from Zone 2. By the same reasoning, there will be no visitors from Zone 3. Thus, at a $1.00 admission fee, there will be 400 visitors—200 from Zone 1 and 200 from Zone 2. This provides us with another point on the demand curve

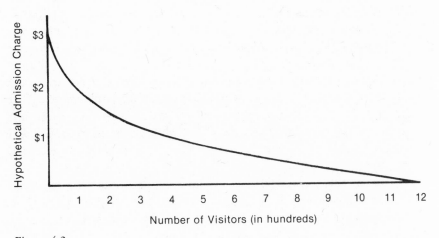

Figure 4-2.

as shown in figure 4-2. Finally, at a $3.00 entrance fee there will be no visitors from any of the zones. This produces still a third point on the diagram—the point at which the quantity demanded will fall to zero.

Obviously, this example is meant to be as simple as possible, and because it established only a few points on the demand curve, would provide only a very rough approximation of an actual curve. But the principle is the same, even in much more complicated applications.

Valuing Agricultural Impacts

Agricultural production, even in the most advanced countries, is heavily influenced by factors that are beyond the producer's control. Within the more industrialized countries, yields have increased more slowly over the past decade than before. This may be partly because of environmental factors induced by humans, possibly including lower air quality, at least in particular regions. Some efforts have been made in the past to calculate yield reductions in such regions, and these reductions have been multiplied by crop prices to estimate the value of lost production. This apparently straightforward procedure applied in the past is, however, too simplistic and very well may lead to deceptive results.

The reason for this is that some particularly high-value agricultural crops, such as vegetables and fruits, tend to be concentrated in particular geographic regions because of their specific climate requirements. Given the concentration of such production, and the known adverse effects of air pollution on vegetables and fruits, one might expect price fluctuations for such commodities in response to changes in air quality. The same might occur with more widely grown field crops if the air pollution effects are widespread. Any reduction of yields due to air pollution may affect consumers and producers of those commodities differently. That is, if the quantity demanded is not very responsive to price for, say, celery, consumers would suffer a net loss, while producers in general will benefit from the increase in the price of celery resulting from the reduction in supply.

This seemingly perverse result invites introduction into the discussion of another basic idea from demand theory. The relationship between changes in quantity demanded and changes in price is called by economists *price elasticity* or *elasticity of demand*. Demand elasticity in quantitative terms is the percentage change in the quantity demanded divided by the percentage change in price. Thus, if price goes up by 1 percent and the quantity goes down by 2 percent, the price elasticity is two, and we say that demand is relatively elastic. If the percentage change in price and the percentage change in quantity are the same, we say that demand elasticity is unitary; and if the percentage change in quantity is less than the percentage change in price, we say that demand is relatively inelastic. If demand is relatively inelastic, a reduction in quantity will increase total revenue of producers—the situation cited above. For example, let us say that the price of a commodity is $10 and that at that price the quantity demanded is 20 units. Therefore, in accordance with the explanation given in chapter 3, the total revenue to sellers would be $200. Now suppose that the quantity purchased drops by 10 percent, that is, to 18 units, when the price rises by 20 percent, that is, to $12. Then the total revenue of sellers would rise by 18 x $12, or $216.

We can illustrate this situation more generally by constructing a hypothetical demand curve for celery. In figure 4-3, area P_2, d, Q_2, 0 is larger than area P_1, c, Q_1, 0. This means that with quantity reduction from Q_1 to Q_2, total revenue increases.

While producer's profits may grow because of the higher price of celery, consumers will lose the consumer's surplus shown by the area (a), (b), (c), and (d) on the diagram. This is the maximum they would be willing to pay to avoid the air pollution. This also illustrates the idea of "derived demand" that was introduced, but not explained, in chapter 2.

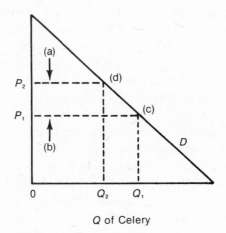

Figure 4-3.

Their willingness to pay for air quality does not stem from the fact that consumers value the air quality directly, but because it is an input to something they do value—celery.

Where price effects of the kind described may be important, it is necessary to develop a method which can properly handle them in the process of analyzing economic losses in agriculture from air pollution. The agricultural component of our research project developed such a method and applied it to southern California (see the case study reported in chapter 9). A different method to handle the same problem for the study of national economic damages to major field crops (reported in chapter 10) is developed and explained there.

Residential Property Values—A Summary Measure?

In an effort to get a summary measure of the value people place on cleaner air, economists have developed a method called the *property value method* for application in *urban* areas. The general idea is to assemble information on all the various characteristics which might determine house price (location, lot size, number of rooms, and other factors), on characteristics of the owner (chiefly income), and on pollution levels at the site studied. Then, by using the statistical technique of regression analysis (explained briefly in chapter 5), it is possible to make an estimate of that part of the difference in house prices which is *separately* associated with differences in air quality at the different sites. Through a procedure which is a bit intricate, and which we need not review here, these estimates can be used to estimate a summed-up (aggregate) "demand" for air quality in the city or metropolitan area being studied. The word, demand, is in quotation marks in the previous sentence because economic theorists have determined that only under a particular set of circumstances can that number be regarded as a valid and accurate estimate of the actual willingness to pay for an improvement in air quality. Nevertheless, the method has some very appealing qualities.

It is relatively inexpensive to do because it can rely on existing data rather than requiring the collection of new data, a process that tends to be quite expensive. That is not to say that existing data are necessarily of high quality, but it can be claimed that the data available for the case studies using this method (see chapter 7) were quite good.

Also, if such an estimate can be regarded as accurate, it provides a quick *summary* measure of the value of air quality to people without having to estimate the value of different characteristics individually. These would include effects on visibility, on soiling and materials damage, and to the extent they are understood, on health.

It would therefore be very useful to run an experiment where demand estimates derived from property-value data are compared with the actual willingness to pay for improvement in air quality. This would permit a test of how importantly the theoretical conditions required to make them precisely equal affect the actual outcomes in practice. It is, of course, impossible to do this, because there is no way to obtain an entirely accurate estimate of willingness to pay. This is illustrated by our discussion of possible biases in bidding games.

What is possible, however, is to compare admittedly imperfect estimates made by both techniques for the same area to test whether they come out pretty close together or yield wildly different results. This is the main point of the South Coast and San Francisco Air Basin studies reported in chapter 7.

References

Blomquist, Glenn. 1979. "Value of Life Saving: Implications of Consumption Activity," *Journal of Political Economy* vol. 87 (June) pp. 540–558.

Smith, R. 1974. "The Feasibility of an 'Injury Tax' Approach to Occupational Safety," *Law and Contemporary Problems* (Summer–Autumn).

Thaler, R., and S. Rosen. 1975. "The Value of Saving a Life: Evidence from the Labor Market," in N. E. Terleckifj, ed., *Household Production and Consumption* (New York, Columbia University Press) pp. 265–297.

II

CASE STUDIES IN URBAN AIR POLLUTION

In the quantitative work done to implement the concepts and procedures discussed in earlier chapters, a number of case studies were undertaken. Their methods and results are presented here and in Part III which deals with rural and regional air and water pollution. The exposure of concentrated populations to air pollution inevitably raises questions about possible health impacts. Chapters 5 and 6 deal with that issue. Chapter 7 discusses the damaging effects of urban air pollution more broadly and is designed primarily to test the comparability of two quite different methodologies for assessing benefits from improved urban air quality—bidding games and property-value studies. Finally, chapter 8 examines the relationship between wage differentials among urban areas and their levels of air pollution as a possible means for evaluating deterioration of air quality.

5

AGGREGATE EPIDEMIOLOGY—THE SIXTY CITIES STUDY

The first study undertaken by the EPA-sponsored research team was concerned with the possible link between air quality and human health. Its objective was to improve estimates of how air pollution may be related to increased risk of death (mortality) from various diseases and to calculate what the economic benefits from reducing this risk might be. As explained earlier, doing this requires three classes of information: (1) establishing the link between ambient conditions and their effects on humans (the dose-response relationship); (2) determining the population at risk; and (3) valuing the economic benefit from improvement in air quality.

The method used to develop the first type of information in this study is called *aggregate epidemiology*. Ideally, in applying epidemiological techniques to the air-quality problem, one would wish to have information about the history of individuals' exposure to air pollution. Furthermore, to isolate the effect of air pollution from other factors influencing health, one would wish information about the individuals' personal characteristics, for example, their age, access to medical care, health-influencing genetic

AUTHOR'S NOTE: This chapter is based primarily on Thomas D. Crocker, William Schulze, Shaul Ben-David, and Allen V. Kneese, *Experiments in the Economics of Air Pollution Epidemiology*, vol. 1 of *Methods Development for Assessing Air Pollution Control Benefits* (Washington, D.C., U.S. Environmental Protection Agency, Office of Health and Ecological Effects, 1979).

factors, dietary habits, whether they smoke, and other pertinent data. At the time the Sixty Cities Study was done, data including this kind of information for individuals were difficult, if not impossible, to get. Accordingly, the researchers often resorted to other more aggregated, and therefore less suitable, data.

For example, in the case study reported here, information pertaining to entire cities was used. That is, total mortality divided by the population for an entire city was used in estimating a dose-response function. This assumes that the average situation can represent individual circumstances and responses. This is a strong assumption which may bias the results of the analysis to an unknown extent.

Other studies have used aggregate epidemiology in an attempt to understand the relationship between air pollution and human health. The study described here differed from the others available at the time it was done in two principal ways. First, it includes factors which are thought to be health-related, but which others had excluded because data were poor or unavailable. These are primarily diet, smoking, and the availability of medical care. Second, in contrast to the usual epidemiological studies, the present study assumes that people do not accept exposure to air pollution passively, but may take actions to avoid its effects. In that sense, it is recognized that there are tradeoffs between air-pollution effects and other values having economic content, for example, incurring the expense of seeing a doctor or of moving away from a polluted city. It is primarily with respect to such economic–behavioral responses that economists can make a contribution to the study of epidemiology. Conventional epidemiology tends to neglect the fact that people have an incentive to adapt to environmental conditions and that they do so. Instead, it treats them as passive acceptors of whatever occurs.

Before discussing these matters further, it may be helpful to readers not familiar with *regression analysis* to say a little about this statistical technique. In doing so, and relating the discussion specifically to the present case, it will be helpful to refer to figure 5-1 below. Along the top is a simple equation which says that mortality is related to (or, as economists say, is a function of) a variety of health-related factors. In such an equation, mortality and the health-related factors are called *variables,* because the data on them may take on a range of different values, depending on the particular situation. For example, where the city is the unit of observation, as in our study, both mortality and air

$$\text{MORTALITY RATE} = F \text{ (MEDICAL CARE, AGE, GENETIC FACTORS, BEHAVIOR AND HABITS, DIET, EXPOSURES)}$$

MORTALITY RATE	MEDICAL CARE,	AGE,	GENETIC FACTORS,	BEHAVIOR AND HABITS,	DIET,	EXPOSURES)
Heart disease	Doctors per capita	Median age	Race	Smoking	Vitamins	Radiation
Cancer	Hospital beds per capita			People per room	Saturated fats	Air pollution
Vascular disease				Race	Cholesterol	Average winter temperature
Pneumonia and influenza					Protein	
Cirrhosis					Additives	
Emphysema and bronchitis					Alcohol	
Kidney disease					Coffee	
Congenital anomalies						
Diseases of early infancy						

Figure 5-1.

pollution differ considerably from city to city. It is these differences that permit regression analysis to work. It can be viewed as a complicated kind of averaging procedure that uses concepts based on statistical probability theory.

The variable on the left-hand side of the equals sign is called the *dependent variable*. This is the variable whose behavior one is trying to explain. The variables on the right-hand side are called the *independent variables,* that is, the ones that are thought to determine what value the dependent variable takes on.

Given the data at hand, the goal of the mathematical manipulations involved in regression analysis is to identify and quantify what separate and independent quantitative effect each of the independent variables has on the dependent variable. One condition for this process to work accurately is that the independent variables must not be interrelated (that is, themselves correlated). This is almost never the case with real data, and for this, as well as some other reasons, there is always more or less uncertainty about the results achieved.

One such instance of interdependency among variables of particular interest in the present study is the effect of medical care on health. The existing epidemiological literature has failed to show any significant effect of medical care on human mortality rates. This result, which most people would not expect, may have a simple explanation. For example, in our analysis of sixty cities, no effect of the availability of doctors on mortality was shown when a straightforward regression was done where the actually observed number of doctors in different cities is entered as one of the independent variables. Although availability of doctors most likely does reduce mortality rates, doctors prefer not to live in polluted cities. Therefore, relative to the total population there are fewer doctors in such cities. Thus, whatever favorable effects doctors have on mortality rates tend to be canceled by their fewer numbers in those cities. Simple regression analysis cannot untangle the relation of doctors to mortality versus the relation of pollution to mortality. This kind of problem is known as *simultaneous equation bias*.

To get to this problem, a "two-stage" regression technique is used in which one first estimates how many doctors there would be in a city aside from the influence of pollution, but with other factors being equal. Then in the second stage, that *estimated* number of doctors is entered into the analysis rather than the *actual* observed number of doctors. This technique *separates* the influence of doctors from the influence of pollution.

This recognition of one aspect of human adaption to pollution had a dramatic effect on the results.

For the full-scale analysis, it was possible to develop for a set of sixty cities the variables shown in figure 5-1. The dietary and smoking variables had to be estimated quite crudely, since no actual observations exist for them. For example, cigarette consumption for a particular city was calculated from cigarette sales tax data for the state in which the city was located. Surely one cannot make any great claims for the quality of these data. It was felt, however, that these variables were potentially so important in influencing health and mortality that to exclude them would be inviting even more serious error.

This leads to a further observation on regression analysis. In the language of the trade, a regression equation must be "specified" properly if one is to have any confidence at all in the result. That means that the "correct" set of variables must be included in the analysis. If all the significant variables are not included in the equation, the equation is misspecified, and a variable that is there may pick up some of the effect actually attributable to one or more of the missing ones. For instance, if smoking is importantly related to health, and if, further, there is a correlation between smoking and air pollution, then if smoking is excluded, there is, so to speak, a surplus effect to be picked up and the air-pollution variable will take some of it.

Let us turn to a discussion of the results of investigating air-quality dose-response relationships. Table 5-1 summarizes the signs the various variables took in regression analysis. Each column represents a regression equation for a possible cause, or set of causes, of mortality. A positive (plus) sign means that an increase in the level of the variable tends to increase mortality, and a negative sign (minus) means that an increase in the level of the variable tends to reduce mortality.

The results shown here are only the "significant" ones. That means that they have passed a purely formal statistical test, but in view of the difficulties of equation specification, simultaneous equation bias, and other problems in application, it does not necessarily mean that they are "true." But if one is confident that the equation is specified about right, and the results for a particular variable are fairly large (and "statistically significant"), it means that we cannot rule out the hypothesis that the relationship is real and nearly the estimated magnitude. Associated with each variable in the regression is a number called a *regression coefficient*. This number is used to quantitatively estimate the change in the dependent

Table 5-1. Summary of Two-Stage Linear Estimates of Factors in Human Mortality Hypotheses Not Rejected at the 97.5 Percent Confidence Level

Variable (sign of hypothetical effect)	Total Mortality Rate	Vascular disease	Heart disease	Pneumonia and influenza	Emphysema and bronchitis	Cirrhosis	Kidney disease	Congenital birth defects	Early infant diseases	Cancer
Doctors per capita[a] (−)	−	−	−		−		−			−
Median age (+)	+	+	+	+		+	+			+
% Nonwhite (+)	+		+			+	+		+	+
Cigarettes (+)	+	+	+							+
Room density (+)	+			+		+				
Cold (+)	+			+			+			+
Animal fat (+)			+							
Protein (+)	+				+					+
Carbohydrates (?)					−					
NO_2 (+)										
SO_2 (+)									+	
Particulates (+)				+						
R^2	.82	.60	.77	.54	.39	.64	.54	.22	.55	.86

[a] Two-stage estimator employed.

variable when the level of the independent variable changes, for example, when air pollution decreases. Since only two calculations have been presented, the reader will not be burdened with all the numbers.

Let us look more closely at the results. Both the median age and percentage of nonwhite variables are widely significant across the estimated variables, and show, as expected, uniformly positive effects on mortality rates.

Cigarette consumption shows significant positive relationships with total mortality, vascular disease, heart disease, and cancer, while room density (that is, the average number of persons per room), and cold (that is, the number of days in which temperature drops below a specified level) both show significant positive relationships with total mortality and pneumonia and influenza. Room density also shows significant positive relationships for cirrhosis and kidney disease.

The dietary variables show significance in total mortality, heart disease, and cancer—relationships between heart disease and saturated fats and between cancer and meat consumption (note the positive association for protein) have long been recognized. The dietary variables also show up as significant in emphysema and bronchitis. Not much credence should be given to the individual dietary variables, because the data are poor and the variables are highly interrelated. Our main concern with diet in this analysis is that we have accounted for diet in a general way in specifying an equation where the primary interest is in the air-pollution variables.

Turning to the air-quality variables, only two significant correlations appear—between particulates and the pneumonia and influenza variable, and between sulfur dioxide and the early infant disease variable. It should be observed that the associations we have found between mortality and air pollution are primarily for diseases of the very young and very old, particularly susceptible groups within the population. Further, the effects are those which one would usually associate with short-term as opposed to long-term air-pollution exposures. We have some confidence in these particular results.

It well may be that aggregate epidemiology may be incapable of revealing the long-term consequences of air-pollution exposures, if they exist. This could be because data are not available on the actual air-pollution exposure of people. In view of changes in environmental conditions and the mobility of the population, current observations of ambient air quality simply may not be an adequate indicator of actual exposure to capture any effects of air pollution on degenerative diseases. For example, cancer may occur as much as two decades after exposure to carcinogenic substances.

Having investigated dose-response relationships, we can turn to an economic evaluation of air-quality control as it pertains to reduced mortality. This analysis is based on the valuation-of-risks approach discussed in chapter 4. As the reader will recall, figures were quoted there which various scholars had obtained by analyzing risky occupations.

First, to obtain national estimates, we must know the population at risk. Since our sixty-city sample is entirely urban, and since air-pollution-related health effects are principally an urban problem, we used a population at health-related risk of 150 million urban dwellers. As a range for the value of reduced risk, we used Thaler's and Rosen's (1975) estimate of $340,000 per life saved as a lower bound, and Smith's (1974) estimate of $1 million as an upper bound. Finally, to get an estimate of reduced risk from air-pollution control, we assumed an average 60 percent reduction in ambient urban concentrations both for sulfur oxides and particulates. Then, using the average concentration of these pollutants in our sixty-city sample as a basis for calculation, we derived an average reduction in risk of pneumonia mortality for a 60 percent reduction in pollution from our estimated dose-response functions for these diseases. It should be noted that this is a very large reduction from present levels, and it would be difficult and very expensive to achieve.

Note, in terms of our discussion in chapter 3, that a more complete analysis would have assumed various levels of control at different *emissions* points, after which a dispersion model would be used to calculate changes in the population at risk and also the levels of risk. These, along with the dose-response estimates and risk valuations, would then be used to calculate associated benefits. We do not yet have the capability of doing this on a national scale. It would be a monumental job to achieve a high level of accuracy in such an undertaking for the entire nation. But this type of capability does exist in various regions.

Multiplying the population at risk by the assumed value of reduced risk, and then by the average reduction in risk, gives a crude approximation of the benefits for a 60 percent reduction in national urban ambient concentrations of particulates and sulfur oxides, respectively.

If the results shown in table 5-2 are accurate—and we cannot vouch for how accurate they may be—they are, in our judgment, conservative with respect to the possible total health effects of air pollution. This is

Table 5-2. Urban Benefits from Reduced Mortality

Disease	Pollutants	Value of reduced risk to 150 million urban residents (billion 1978 $/year)
Pneumonia	Particulates	4.4–13.7
Early infant disease	SO$_2$	0.7–2.2
Total		5.1–15.9

Source: Based on Thomas D. Crocker, William Schulze, Shaul Ben-David, and Allen V. Kneese, *Experiments in the Economics of Air Pollution Epidemiology,* vol. 1 of *Methods Development for Assessing Air Pollution Control Benefits* (Washington, D.C., EPA, 1979).

because we believe that air pollution may well have long-term chronic health effects (and some evidence supporting that is established in chapter 6), but that, given the available data, aggregate epidemiology cannot dependably establish them. Moreover, while this study explicitly recognizes the specification problem, and has made some progress in dealing with it, it does not address the problem in a fully systematic manner. This creates further uncertainty about the accuracy of results. In chapter 6, I turn to a more recent study that would seem capable of yielding much more reliable results.

References

Smith, R. 1974. "The Feasibility of an "Injury Tax' Approach to Occupational Safety," *Law and Contemporary Problems* (Summer–Autumn).

Thaler, R., and S. Rosen. 1975. "The Value of Saving a Life: Evidence from the Labor Market," in N. E. Terleckifj, ed., *Household Production and Consumption* (New York, Columbia University Press) pp. 265–297.

6

DISAGGREGATE EPIDEMIOLOGY AND MORBIDITY FROM OZONE EXPOSURE

The most general conclusion to be drawn from the experiment with aggregate epidemiology discussed in chapter 5, and from review of the work of others, is that the results of such studies, if accurate at all, are so only within very wide bounds. It appears that only observations on individuals could improve the situation. We refer to epidemiology using econometric techniques such as regression analysis, and performed on data about individual persons, as *microepidemiology*. The objective of the microepidemiology study reported here was to examine a possible link between exposure to ozone and health damage. The known physiological effects of ozone suggest that such a link could exist.

For this purpose, a great effort was expended to build a suitable data base. (The general term *data base* usually is used to refer to an assembly of quantitative information that is suitable for analysis.) In order to do so the researchers merged the information in two existing sets of data that have recently become available. The first is the 1979 Health Interview Survey (HIS) data assembled by the National Center for Health Statistics.

AUTHOR'S NOTE: This chapter is based primarily on Paul R. Portney and John Mullahy, "Ambient Ozone and Human Health: An Epidemiological Analysis," vols. I and II, Draft Final Report, prepared under Grant no. 68-02-3583 for the U.S. Environmental Protection Agency, Economic Analysis Branch, Office of Air Quality Planning and Standards (Research Triangle Park, N.C., September 1983).

The second is 1979 air pollution data from the Environmental Protection Agency's monitoring system. The resulting data base contains a very large number of observations, a situation which, as we will see shortly, has a number of advantages.

The HIS was started in 1957 and has been conducted annually since then. A sample of about 110,000 people, located across the country, is interviewed every year. Information pertinent to epidemiological study is obtained, including:

1. Demographic characteristics (including age, income, sex, occupation, and others)

2. Number of days during the two-week period prior to the survey on which the respondent had to restrict his or her activity, stay in bed, and miss work or school

3. Visits to doctors or dentists during this two-week period

4. Acute and chronic health conditions (including some diagnostic information) accounting for restricted activity or doctor visits

5. Hospital episodes during the twelve-month period prior to the interview

6. Smoking habits, history of residential mobility (especially detailed information was elicited in the 1979 survey), home health-care utilization, vaccination history, eye care, and retirement income.

As far as air pollution data are concerned, information was collected from the EPA's system on ambient concentration for eight major pollutants for 1979. Using a program that matches individual census tracts to the nearest air-pollution monitor, it is possible to assign each individual in the HIS the air-pollution readings nearest to his or her home. While this still does not provide an accurate measure of an individual's dose, it is clearly superior to the assumption that an entire city is subject to the same exposure, a device that had to be resorted to in the macroepidemiological study reported on in the previous chapter. Also, the data set permitted matching of individual health status to air-quality conditions prevailing for two or three weeks prior to the interview as well as to annual averages and other periods. This is important when identifying acute effects.

The final data set contained about 14,500 adults and about 15,700 children. These were persons who could be matched with air-quality monitors and for whom smoking information could be obtained. In chapter 5, it was pointed out that one of the factors limiting macroepidemiological analysis is the mobility of the population, which means that exposure at their current address often reflects long-term exposure only very poorly. A supplement to the 1979 HIS interviews provides information on persons who have resided at the same location for a long period. The large size of the whole sample permits these persons, whose exposure history can be defined more accurately, to be studied separately.

An unfortunate aspect of the data set is that it does not permit study of the possible link between air pollution and mortality, the relationship analyzed in the macroepidemiological studies. Therefore, direct comparisons of the two approaches are not possible. But the data set does contain information about the presence or absence of chronic respiratory, cardiovascular, and other illnesses. Thus, it is possible to test the proposition that air pollutants not only may induce acute health effects, but may be related to the development or prolongment of chronic conditions which may lead to earlier mortality.

Another advantage of the very large data set is that effects on children, asthmatics, or other potentially sensitive people can be tested. Other efforts to do this have been hampered by small sample size. Many such subsamples were analyzed to test the sensitivity of results to the kind of group selected. For example, some public health specialists believe that environmental pollutants could have an especially adverse effect on children. Experiments to test this hypothesis were done, and they did not confirm it in the case of ozone. Accordingly, the remainder of this chapter focuses on the attempt to identify impacts on the entire set of adults.

In accordance with information available from the HIS surveys, the researchers tried to identify relationships between ozone levels and four primary dependent variables (recall the discussion of dependent and independent variables in chapter 5). Three have to do with acute illness: these are "restricted-activity days," "work-loss days," and "bed-disability days." Finally, the researchers examined the information for a link between ozone and "chronic respiratory disease." The *independent* variables in general resembled those used in the Sixty Cities Study (see chapter 5), for example, age, sex, income, and smoking habits, among others, except that in this instance, they pertain to actual individuals in the sample rather than being averaged across entire cities. Having information about individuals also permitted the researchers to introduce other variables which could influence morbidity. One of these, labeled "FAT" in the computer study, was meant to represent the person's general physical condition. It was possible only to construct a crude proxy, and this consisted of weight in pounds divided by height in inches. The hypothesis was that being excessively underweight or overweight might be associated with higher morbidity. In general, results of the analysis supported this view.

One independent variable that deserves special note in the analysis of acute morbidity is "chronic illness." Here the hypothesis is that persons who have a chronic disease may be more subject to episodes of acute morbidity than those who do not. Again, the analysis conducted is consistent with this supposition. Of course, in each instance, ozone levels at the appropriate monitoring stations for each individual were included among the independent variables, as were readings for the other air pollutants.

The method used in identifying the separate effect of each of these independent variables on the dependent morbidity variables was once again the regression analysis explained in chapter 5. A number of experiments were conducted with regression equations, including different variables (specifications) and different subsamples of the whole sample.

As one would expect from the discussion in chapter 5, the results were sensitive to the specification used. For example, the calculated effect of ozone on health was often influenced by what other pollution variables were included in the equation, for example, particulate matter.

But for the acute morbidity variables—restricted-activity days, work-loss days, and bed-disability days—the relation between them and ozone readings was almost always positive and, in many cases, significant in the purely formal statistical sense. Econometricians refer to a variable that behaves in this consistent manner across experiments as being "robust." Robustness in the uncertain world of statistical analysis gives one some confidence that what is being observed in the data is real. Although the researchers find some very tentative evidence to support it, the relationship between ozone levels and chronic respiratory disease is less robust and therefore leaves one in greater doubt as to its genuine existence.

Thus, even epidemiology conducted with information on individuals and with much better exposure data than is available for macroepide-miology does not yield the clean and persuasive results one would wish and hope for.

With these cautions in mind, let us turn to some sample results concerning the changes in health status that a change in ozone levels might yield. Once a relationship between independent and dependent variables has been estimated, it is then possible to hypothetically change the value of an independent variable and, using this quantitative relationship, calculate the associated change in the dependent variable. For example, one can reduce the observed ozone level and calculate the effect on, say, restricted-activity days.

I will present the results from two of the many equations estimated. These may be taken to be representative of those in which the association between ozone and health indicators was positive and significant in the statistical sense.

The first illustration is an equation which tries to establish an association between ozone and restricted-activity days (RAD). It is specified as follows:

RAD = F(ozone, sulfates, race, sex, marital status, income, urban,
        FAT, age, smoking, education, chronic health condition,
        crowding, temperature, precipitation, humidity)

In this equation, ozone and several other independent variables—for example, income and chronic disease—meet the statistical significance test, but most of the others do not. As an unexplained anomaly, the sulfate variable is negative and significant. This has the hardly credible implication that sulfate pollution is good for you.

If one takes the ozone result at face value, it indicates that each .01 part-per-million (ppm) increase in the highest hourly reading for a day could result in 0.025 more RADs per person over a two-week period. (Recall that respondents to the HIS survey were asked to report on their health status for the two weeks immediately prior to the survey.) Or conversely, a smiliar decrease in ozone would result in a similar decrease in RADs. If this result is extrapolated to a whole year, it means that .01-ppm reduction in ozone would result in 0.65 fewer RADs, on the average, per person per year. Extrapolating further to a population of about 110 million adults (over seventeen) in the metropolitan areas of the United States implies about 70 million fewer RADs for the country, associated with the ozone decrease. Portney and Mullahy made no effort to assign an economic value to this environmental improvement, but it is immediately apparent that the per-day value would not have to be large to yield an impressive annual benefit. If, for example, the consumers surplus from avoiding a RAD were a mere $10 per day, the aggregate national benefit would be about $700 million per year.

The other illustrative results pertain to the possible effect of ozone on chronic respiratory disease (CRD). The equation specification for this analysis was:

$$CRD = F(\text{ozone, suspended particulates, sulfur oxide, race, sex,}$$
$$\text{marital status, income, FAT, age, smoking, education,}$$
$$\text{temperature, precipitation, humidity})$$

In this case in addition to ozone, sulfur dioxide SO_2 or SO_4 (this time positive, but small), race, sex, income, age, education, and humidity were significant in the statistical sense.

If one goes through calculations like those outlined for RAD above, the results show that .01-ppm reduction in the average annual hourly ozone concentration across the country would cause the incidence of CRD to gradually evolve to a point where there would be about 1,130,000 fewer cases per year. If one assumes that the consumer surplus associated with avoiding one case of CRD is only $1,000, the .01-ppm reduction would ultimately yield benefits of greater than $1 billion a year. The full benefits are not available immediately because chronic disease lags exposure change by some years.

There are several things to be said about these results: first, while .01 ppm is, from an everday perspective, a very small number, it is large compared to the actually existing average levels of ozone. It implies about a 20 percent decrease from the average daily maximum reading around the country and a 50 percent decrease from the average hourly reading. It should be noted that such a decrease would be difficult and costly to achieve. It is not necessarily obvious that, even if the benefit numbers quoted above were true, the economic benefits would outweigh the costs.

Second, as noted, the results are rather robust with respect to the statistical linkage between ozone and acute morbidity. It does not seem unreasonable to argue that this provides support for the view that there is a significant real link. The results with respect to chronic respiratory disease are not robust and therefore have to be doubted.

Third, in general the results of the macro- and microepidemiology studies reported here, and related work of others, do not foreclose the possibility that health benefits from reducing air pollution are large. But the exact, or even approximate, magnitude of those benefits is far from being established.

7

AIR-QUALITY BENEFITS IN THE SOUTH COAST AIR BASIN AND IN SAN FRANCISCO

For the household sector, and considering other factors in addition to health, two distinct approaches to valuation of environmental quality have emerged from recent research. The first, as explained in chapter 4, involves the analysis of how some pertinent actual market prices, such as real property prices, are influenced by environmental quality attributes of the properties. The second, also discussed in chapter 4, tries to induce individuals to reveal directly their actual preferences in monetary terms for environmental attributes. Clearly, if these methods are valid, there should be a well-defined relationship between what people do pay through differences in property values and what they say they will pay, provided that there are no incentives for them to distort their bids and that influences other than air quality on property values are correctly accounted for.

AUTHOR'S NOTE: This chapter is based primarily on David S. Brookshire, Ralph C. d'Arge, William D. Schulze, and Mark A. Thayer, *Experiments in Valuing Nonmarket Goods: A Case Study of Alternative Benefit Measures of Air Pollution Control in the South Coast Air Basin,* vol. 2 of *Methods Development for Assessing Air Pollution Control Benefits* (Washington, D.C., U.S. Environmental Protection Agency, Office of Health and Ecological Effects, Office of Research and Development, 1979); and on Edna Loehman, David Boldt, and Kathleen Chaikin, *Study Design and Property Value Study,* vol. 1 of *Measuring the Benefits of Air Quality Improvements in the San Francisco Bay Area* (Menlo Park, Calif., SRI International, 1980).

The South Coast Air Basin Study

The first area where these techniques were tested and compared in our study—the South Coast Air Basin—consists of Orange and Los Angeles counties and portions of San Bernadino and Riverside counties of California. This area has a long history of air-quality problems. For instance, Spanish explorers in the sixteenth century noted smoke from Indian campfires in the Basin, trapped by inadequate horizontal and vertical air mixing. The period immediately following World War II, which saw extremely rapid population growth in southern California accompanied by massive industrial development, was marked by the appearance of smog as the major threat to the regional environment. As a result, air-pollution-abatement programs began in the late 1960s as a response to the discovery of the automobile's role in smog formation. Deterioration of air quality in the South Coast Air Basin has multiple causes: unfavorable topography and meteorology, and dense population and economic activity with corresponding large emissions.

To conduct the study, a special sampling procedure was developed. It was designed to identify paired communities in the Basin that are similar in as many ways possible except in air quality. If the other characteristics of these communities are not very different across areas (housing styles, sizes, distance to the beach, and other factors), the difference in property values between an area characterized by clean air versus an area where air quality is lower should be due mostly to the existence or absence of pollution. This structured, paired-communities sampling procedure, rather than a random sample of individuals over the whole region, was chosen *primarily* to control for proximity to the beach. Nearness to the ocean and cleaner air are so highly correlated that the most applicable statistical procedure, regression analysis, performed on a random sample would not be able to distinguish these two major influences on house prices in southern California.

The Los Angeles area was chosen for the initial experiment not only because of its well-defined air-pollution problem, but also because of the existence of excellent property-value data. Twelve census tracts were chosen for sampling for both the property-value and the companion bidding-game study. For the latter, interviews were conducted in these tracts during March 1978. Respondents were asked to state their willingness to pay for an improvement in air quality at their current location. Air quality was defined as poor, fair, or good, based both on maps of the region (the pollution gradient across the area is both well defined and well understood by local residents) and on photographs of a distant vista representative of the differing air-quality levels. Households in poor air-quality areas were asked to value an improvement to fair air quality, and those in fair areas were asked to value an improvement to good air quality. A total of 290 completed surveys was obtained. Figure 7-1 shows the areas having poor-, fair-, and good-quality air in the South Coast Air Basin.

Built into the survey questionnaire were procedures for identifying the various possible biases in bidding games (see chapter 4). No biases were found. The results indicate that, on the average, households said they were willing to pay $30 per month more for cleaner air. For comparison to the survey responses, data were obtained on 634 single-family home sales which occurred between January 1977 and March 1978 in the paired communities used for the survey analysis. Households will choose to locate somewhere along a pollution–property-value gradient, paying

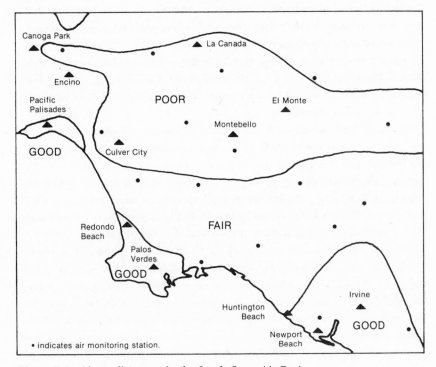

Figure 7-1. Air quality areas in the South Coast Air Basin.

more, other attributes being equal, for homes in areas with clean air, depending on their family income and tastes. However, economic reasoning suggests that the cost difference between homes in two different air-quality areas will exceed the willingness to pay as elicited by a bidding game for a similar improvement in air quality. Thus, we would expect house-cost differences associated with air-quality improvement to exceed estimates of household willingness to pay from the survey responses. This is because property values at a particular location will reflect the air-quality preferences of the most air-quality-sensitive individuals, whereas average bids for that same air quality will more nearly reflect the average preferences of persons living there. Most houses are not for sale at a given time, but given the small number available, their price will be determined by those who want them most, for example, those people with the strongest preference for cleaner air.

A straightforward statistical comparison of the paired neighborhoods indicates that property-value differences between localities with poor and fair air quality are about $140 per household when computed on a monthly basis. Using more advanced economic models—which better take into account factors other than pollution, such as any remaining influence of distance to ocean and differences in tastes which also may influence property values—willingness to pay inferred from the property-value differences is about $40 per month. As a reasonably comparable estimate, the survey results, as indicated, show an average bid of slightly less than $30 per month.

The results indicate that air-quality deterioration in the Los Angeles area has had substantial effects on housing prices and that these are comparable to what people say they are willing to pay for improved air quality. Moreover, the property-value estimates are higher than the average bids, which, as noted above, was expected on theoretical grounds.

Based on these results, rough estimates can be made about willingness to pay for improved air quality throughout the South Coast Air Basin. Difficulties are encountered in making data sets for groups of diverse households exactly comparable. Significant differences exist between the people in the survey and the property-value groups in average income, age, and other socioeconomic factors. Accordingly, any extrapolation to the Basin as a whole must be taken as rather crude and merely indicative rather than exact.

Shown below are estimates of monthly bids for cleaner air by households,

30 Percent improvement in air quality	Value per survey area household per month (in 1977$)	Annual benefits (in billions of 1977$) for the South Coast Air Basin
Property value study		
Based on straightforward comparison of communities	135	3.96
Calculated willingness to pay, taking account of other factors	42	0.95
Survey study		
Mean bid	29	0.65

results of the property-value study, and extrapolation of the benefits for an approximate 30 percent improvement in air quality within the South Coast Air Basin. The last estimate, while quite rough, does suggest that economic benefits from an improvement in air quality in the South Coast Air Basin are very large.

The results of this experiment also suggest that survey instruments, when compared with property-value techniques, may provide a reasonable way to obtain environmental quality benefit estimates. The survey approach has the advantage that new data can be collected at low cost on specific environmental problems. The investigator is not tied to the availability of existing data sets which are usually not designed to meet his or her particular needs.

As a caution, however, it should be kept in mind that the South Coast Air Basin studies were conducted in an area where an individual has both an exceptionally clear-cut pollution situation that he or she has personally experienced and access to a well-developed property-value market for clean air. The effect of clean air on property values and, in turn, on the degree to which people are aware of increased housing prices in good air-quality areas appears to be exceptionally well-defined in the South Coast Air Basin. Therefore, it should be recognized that the results of this experiment well may not carry over completely to other situations where air quality is not so well specified, either through actual market prices or by the perceptions of those interviewed.

The San Francisco Bay Area Study

In view of the possible uniqueness of the Los Angeles Basin, a follow-up study was done replicating as much as practical the Los Angeles study. The place chosen was the San Francisco Bay area. This is a large shallow basin ringed by hills stretching from southern Marin to Santa Clara counties. The basin tapers into a series of sheltered valleys including Santa Clara, Livermore, and Napa. While the area typically has better ventilation than the Los Angeles Basin, its topography gives the area great potential for trapping and accumulating air pollutants.

Figure 7-2 shows the study area. The numbers on the lines indicate increasingly higher levels of smog pollution.

As in the case of Los Angeles, both property values as they related to levels of pollution and a questionnaire technique were applied. These were compared with each other, given the hypotheses explained earlier, and to the Los Angeles results. Let us turn first to the property-value study.

While the intention was to make the two studies as comparable as possible, there were some inevitable differences in both the situations and in the data available that made some adaptations necessary. For example, in southern California, as suggested, the mild year-round climate encourages a variety of ocean-related recreational activities. Beachfront activity is highly valued, and beachfront property has generally been densely developed. In the San Francisco area, the Bay is the most accessible body of water to major population centers; however, the Bay does not offer the same scenic or recreational experiences found along the coast of the Los Angeles area. In the Bay area, oceanfront property is located over the ridge of the Santa Cruz Mountains and is less accessible to the major employment centers. As a result, much of the beachfront property has a rural atmosphere.

Accordingly, it was not necessary to adopt the paired-communities approach of the Los Angeles study to control for access to the beach. This made a more nearly random sampling approach possible, which has the advantage of providing a more dependable basis for extrapolating the sample results to the entire area.

Another principal difference between the areas is air quality. Although photochemical smog (oxidant pollution) is considered to be the major problem in both regions, the city of San Francisco has a less severe air-pollution problem than Los Angeles. However, some cities included in

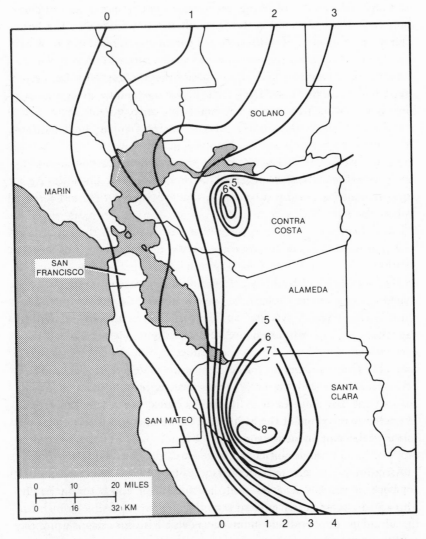

Figure 7-2. Expected annual ozone levels in the San Francisco Bay Area exceeding the federal ozone standard in 1978, in days per year with a high hourly average exceeding 0.12 ppm, based on a three-year average (1976–78). Based on data from Edna Loehman, David Boldt, and Kathleen Chaikin, *Study Design and Property Value Study,* vol. 1 of *Measuring the Benefits of Air Quality Improvements in the San Francisco Bay Area* (Menlo Park, Calif., SRI International, 1980).

the region (San Jose and Los Gatos, for example) suffer from severe pollution problems.

Thus, while the San Francisco region provides suitable contrast in air quality from place to place, still air-quality degradation is not in general so severe and, one would expect, possibly not so well defined in people's minds. Accordingly, it was judged to be an excellent place to see whether the Los Angeles results would hold up in this different situation.

Data on property values were gathered or constructed for 2,500 households in the region. These same households subsequently were used for interviewing. In addition, data were collected on about 5,000 residential property sales in areas where these families live. Unfortunately, the sales data available for San Francisco were not as accurate as the Los Angeles data. The data were used in regression analyses in an attempt to isolate the effects of degraded air from other factors affecting air quality, such as income of residents, house characteristics, and access to work places.

Results of the San Francisco study as compared with the South Coast Air Basin study were in accordance with the hypotheses made about them.

First, one would expect a 30 percent improvement in air quality to yield less benefit per capita in an area where the air is already relatively clean. Two types of results from the San Francisco study support this supposition: (1) a 30 percent improvement in air quality yields a much larger benefit estimate, by both the property value and survey method, for the dirtiest subarea in the San Francisco region than the average for the region as a whole; and (2) a 30 percent improvement in air quality, again as estimated by both techniques, yields an average benefit estimate between five and six times as high in the Los Angeles region as it does in the San Francisco region.

Second, one would anticipate more variability of results from subarea to subarea within a region (San Francisco) where the pollution problem is both less intense and less well defined than in the Los Angeles area. Again, this supposition is borne out.

As before, on theoretical grounds, one would suppose that the property-value study would yield higher estimates of benefits than the survey approach. As in the South Coast Air Basin, this expectation is met in the San Francisco study, and the relationship between the two alternative estimates is about the same as in the former.

Accordingly, the two studies have a broad consistency in that the differences in their findings are expected differences. In general, the San Francisco study supports the conclusion of the Los Angeles study that survey instruments may provide a reasonable, low-cost way to obtain benefit estimates of environmental quality.

An Illustrative Benefit–Cost Analysis

While the basic purpose of the studies reported on in this part was to develop improved methods for evaluating the *benefits* from air-quality improvement or maintenance, an illustrative *benefit–cost* analysis was also done. This is included simply to show how benefits estimation fits into the economic analysis of environmental policy. Not much credence should be accorded the actual numbers. The subject of the study was the benefits and costs of meeting national ambient standards in the South Coast Air Basin. Selection of this area, aside from its intrinsic importance, permitted use of the information developed for the benefits study reported earlier in this chapter.

The national ambient standards for oxidants (a 0.12-ppm maximum hourly concentration—since the study was completed, the basis for the standard has been changed from oxidants to ozone) and nitrogen dioxide (a 0.05-ppm annual average concentration) are consistently violated throughout the Basin with the notable exception of the immediate coastal areas, which were characterized as having "good" air quality. Accordingly, if the entire South Coast Air Basin were to be brought into compliance with ambient standards, areas that in the earlier study were characterized as having "fair" or "poor" air quality would then be characterized as having "good" air quality. The development of an aggregate-benefit measure for achieving ambient standards (note that this is a different objective from the 30 percent improvement assumed in the earlier study) for the entire basin is then done by extrapolation. Benefits are taken to be the aggregate willingness to pay for all households in both "poor" and "fair" air-quality areas to have "good" air quality, as defined for both the property-value and survey studies.

In making the necessary benefits estimates, the property-value results were the ones actually used. These results allow calculation of household willingness to pay as related to income and air pollution. It is this relationship that was used for benefit calculations. It assumes that income and population affect willingness to pay for air-quality improvement in the same way throughout the Basin as they did in the limited sample. The estimates are strictly for household willingness to pay and exclude any agricultural and ecosystem effects. (See chapter 8 for a discussion of agricultural benefits for the area.)

Since benefits were calculated for moving from the current level of air quality (1976 emissions inventory) to the ambient standards, costs must be calculated on the same basis. However, analysis indicated that costs for on-road mobile-source control measures were substantially better done than those associated with stationary source controls. Therefore, only the costs attributable to on-road mobile-source control were examined in the study. The benefits that are counted are then only those corresponding to the share of total emissions reductions which are accomplished by mobile-source control.

Although a careful engineering cost study of using mobile-source control to achieve ambient standards would have been desirable, the objective of the study was, as noted, mostly illustrative, and resources for it were quite limited. The researchers therefore were forced to use cost estimates found in the literature. Unfortunately, in many cases these are quite uncertain. For the most part, manufacturers' statements and government publications were relied upon for cost calculations.

In addition, the Southern California Association of Governments' *Air Quality Management Plan* was the basis for the calculation of required emissions reductions—the necessary "link" between emissions and ambient conditions discussed in chapter 3. Calculations presented in the plan indicate that to achieve ambient standards in 1979 would require reductions of about 975 tons per day in reactive hydrocarbons, about 6,000 tons per day of carbon monoxide, and about 500 tons per day of nitrogen oxides. Of these amounts, it was estimated that mobile-source controls are responsible for about 730 tons per day, all of the reduction, and about 400 tons per day of hydrocarbons, carbon monoxide, and oxides of nitrogen, respectively.

Applying these methods and data, it was found that benefits of achieving ambient standards for air quality in the South Coast Air Basin for 1979 fall in a range of $1.5 to $3.0 billion per year (note this is a much larger improvement than the 30 percent reported on page 64). Of this total, on-road mobile-source control would be responsible for approximately $1.4 to $2.6 billion. The corresponding total basinwide control costs fall in the range of $600,000 to $1.32 billion. It therefore appears, with due regard to all the many uncertainties involved, that the benefits of achieving mobile-source controls in the South Coast Air Basin could outweigh the costs. One of the main uncertainties is whether the reductions in the emissions postulated would actually meet the ambient standards. If larger emissions reductions were actually required, costs would rise rapidly.

8

AIR QUALITY, WAGES, AND NATIONAL BENEFITS FROM URBAN AIR-POLLUTION CONTROL

As indicated in previous chapters, one line of study in searching for improved methods to estimate benefits of air quality is to look for actual human responses, reflected in prices of things, that might give a clue as to how much people value clean air. Application of the property-value approach discussed in chapter 7 is one such effort. This approach is based on the idea that people's choices of residence reflect the ambient air quality as well as a number of other characteristics of particular sites.

Another way in which human behavior, reflected in a price, might display preferences with respect to air pollution is the differences in compensation that people might demand for performing particular jobs at different locations with differing air-pollution characteristics. The idea is that, in considering job and location choices, workers will take into account pollution in the area as well as other workplace characteristics. One of the studies in the work being discussed here was designed to test this idea.

AUTHOR'S NOTE: This chapter is based on material from Shaul Ben-David, Reza Pazand, Thomas D. Crocker, Ralph C. d'Arge, Shelby Gerking, and William Schulze, "Six Studies of Health Benefits from Air Pollution Control," vol. 2; and David S. Brookshire, William D. Schulze, Ralph C. d'Arge, Thomas D. Crocker, and Shelby Gerking, with Mark A. Thayer, "Six Studies on Nonmarket Valuation Techniques," vol. 3 of *Methods Development for Environmental Control Benefits Assessment* (Washington, D.C., U.S. Environmental Protection Agency, n.d.).

As is, unfortunately, always the case in this game, the data available for doing the analysis are far from ideal. A basic source of information used was the Panel Study of Income Dynamics, sponsored by the Survey Research Center at the University of Michigan. This study yielded usable wage information on nearly 1,400 heads of households across the country. The information obtained in this survey included the head of household's state and county of residence and type of employment. The location information permitted the matching of other information about variables, one of which might be pollution, that might influence real (that is, price-correlated) wages. As in the case of the epidemiology study described in chapter 5, a set of independent variables was specified that was thought to influence wages, data about them were developed, and the regression technique was used in an attempt to estimate the separate influence of each of them on wages.

The general form of the equation used was as follows:

Wage = F [whether the individual is a union member, whether the individual is a veteran, the size of the individual's family, the individual's health status, the individual's education, the length of time the individual has spent on his or her present job, the climate in the individual's area of residence, job hazards, and levels of pollution—sulfur dioxide, total suspended particulates (that is, fine microscopic particles), and nitrogen dioxide].

Of all of the independent variables, the worst-quality data is for the air-pollution variables. This is because some of the measurement procedures are not very dependable, and because, in some areas, the pollution data are available only on a countywide basis or none of the monitoring stations is located near the individual's workplace.

Further, uncertainty about the accuracy of results comes from the fact that, because of data limitation, it was not possible to include all variables that might influence wages. For example, the availability of recreational opportunities and social services might influence wage rates. If variables are excluded that have an important influence, we know that the results may be biased. In chapter 5, the specification problem was discussed more extensively in connection with its role in epidemiology analysis.

These qualifications having been made, the results of the analysis show that only total suspended particulates are statistically significantly related to wages. Estimating this relationship and that of other variables that influence wages can be used to determine the damage avoided (benefit) of reducing suspended particulates in particular urban areas. This is done by adding to the equation the actual observed value of all the other independent variables for that metropolitan area except that the standard for particulates is substituted for the actual concentration. Then calculations are made of the implications for wages using the regression relationships computed from national data. This result is then adjusted for the population of the particular metropolitan area.

This kind of calculation was done for the Denver and the Cleveland metropolitan areas. The resulting total benefits per year for Denver were about $240 million and for Cleveland about $70 million.[1]

An attractive feature of the methodology just described is that it is fairly straightforward and adaptable to producing a national estimate of the benefits of pollution control. It is a relatively simple matter to make an estimate of the type described above for each metropolitan area in the United States and then to add them up to form a national benefits total. But doing so would have required more data collection and calculation than was possible at the time.

A *very* rough approximation of this procedure can, however, be done as follows: First, one assumes that the situation in Denver is characteristic of metropolitan areas in the West, and that of Cleveland is similar to conditions in the East. Then one computes the per-capita benefits for each metropolitan area and multiplies the result times the total population of the western and eastern metropolitan areas, respectively. When these calculations are done, an estimate of yearly benefits of meeting secondary standards of about $5 billion is obtained for the West, about $4 billion for the East, and about $9 billion for meeting the secondary standard for suspended particulates everywhere. This is, of course, an exceedingly crude procedure, and the amounts given are simply meant to be illustrative of the method.

If these figures have any validity at all, we presume that what is being measured is primarily the more visible and tangible aspects of air quality—visibility and soiling—rather than human health effects. If this is so, the benefits to health from a large improvement in air quality should be added to these estimates. In chapter 5, we estimated that such

---

[1]These results are roughly consistent with those found in a related study by another member of the research team—Maureen Cropper (1980).

benefits could range between about $5 and $16 billion per year. If this range is also accepted, our total estimated *urban* benefit from a large improvement in air quality might be between $15 and $30 billion per year.

Although the basis for these figures is scandalously weak, and they cannot be put forward as genuine estimates but only as illustrative of methods, I do not necessarily find them incredible. For example, in the relatively more carefully done studies in the South Coast Air Basin (see chapter 7), annual benefits from a large improvement in air quality were, as estimated for the benefit–cost study, in the range of $1.5 to $3 billion. If we compare this to the higher of the two national estimates, it does not seem unlikely that benefits in Los Angeles could be 5 to 10 percent of the total. While metropolitan Los Angeles has about 2 percent of the U.S. population, it also has the nation's most severe and widespread air pollution problem. It does seem unlikely, however, that the Los Angeles area could have as much as 10 to 20 percent of the benefit from a large improvement in national air quality to meet ambient air quality standards and protect health. It therefore seems unlikely, based on this slender bit of evidence, that the number given is an overestimate of national urban air-quality benefits.

It should be noted in closing that some, possibly important, benefits are not captured, or not fully captured, by the methods and data presently available. An example is materials damage, which could be quite large.

Finally, the reader should be reminded that the central objective of the research reported in this book is to improve the methods rather than make actual estimates. Any numbers presented in the text must be appropriately discounted in light of that fact.

Reference

Cropper, Maureen, "Inter-City Wage Differentials and the Value of Air Quality," *Journal of Urban Economics* (September) 1980.

III

CASE STUDIES IN RURAL AND REGIONAL AIR AND WATER POLLUTION

The urban cases reviewed in Part II are instances in which one wishes to know the benefits of improving an existing degraded condition. The first four cases reviewed in Part III are also of that type. They concern southern California agriculture and the effect of ozone on U.S. agriculture (chapter 9), and freshwater fishing and national benefits from improvements in water quality (chapter 10). But there are also important air- and water-pollution issues that raise the question of what it is worth to protect a relatively pristine area. Chapter 11 discusses the protection of visibility in the national parks, the prevention of groundwater contamination, and the safeguarding of parts of the ecosystem against damage from acid rain.

9

EFFECT OF AIR QUALITY ON U.S. AGRICULTURE

The Southern California Study

As indicated in chapter 3, agricultural production is affected by many influences beyond the control of individual producers. In agricultural regions within, or nearby, urban areas, air pollution has, in recent decades, become one of these influences. As discussed in chapter 4, when these agricultural regions—say, because of unique climate characteristics—dominate the national or regional production of selected crops, output price increases may occur when air pollution reduces crop yields. In turn, these price increases will reduce the well-being of consumers. In addition, if increases in market prices are insufficient to offset reduction in output (demand is relatively elastic), producers also may be made worse off. On the other hand, if demand is relatively inelastic, they will be made better off. Consumers, however, are always made worse off.

Seasonally (mainly in winter and in spring), southern California produces a major share of the nation's vegetables and fruits. Also, large volumes

AUTHOR'S NOTE: This section is based primarily on Richard M. Adams, Narongsdakdi Thanavibulchai, and Thomas D. Crocker, *A Preliminary Assessment of Air Pollution Damages for Selected Crops Within Southern California,* vol. 3 of *Methods Development for Assessing Air Pollution Control Benefits* (Washington, D.C., U.S. Environmental Protection Agency, Office of Health and Ecological Effects, Office of Research and Development, 1979).

of field crops such as cotton and sugar beets are grown in the region. Smog that periodically blankets the region and its adverse biological effects on many of these crops are well documented. Few attempts have been made to assess the economic impacts of these effects, and those that have been simply multiply the estimated reductions in yields by a constant price (see chapter 4). As we have seen, this method is especially inappropriate for crops having geographically concentrated production patterns, since their market prices will vary with the quantity available from the region. Furthermore, the method is unable to account for changes in cropping patterns that may be induced in response to pollution. This difficulty resembles that of standard epidemiology which, as explained in chapter 5, does not account for human economic responses and adaptations to pollution.

In the research presented here, a more general and powerful methodology has been employed to assess the economic impact of air pollution upon fourteen annual vegetable and field crops in four agricultural subregions of central and southern California. These subregions are shown in figure 9-1. The researchers have included an analysis of changes in comparative

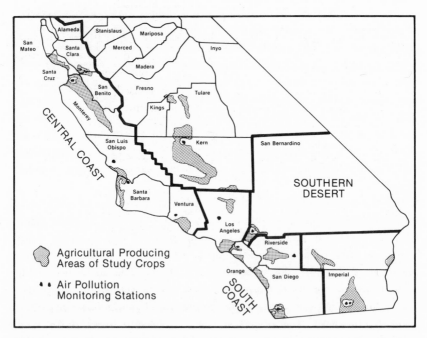

Figure 9-1. Agricultural producing areas in the study. Dots indicate air-pollution-monitoring stations.

economic advantages between, and among, crops and growing locations in response to increased air pollution. In addition, the method used makes it possible to distinguish between the impact upon consumers and that upon producers of these air pollution-induced changes.

The particular method used in this analysis is called *mathematical programming*. This is a type of economic modeling analysis which, given information about available technologies and about the costs of inputs and the demands for outputs, can be used to find the maximum value for an economic objective. For example, in the case of a private business, this procedure might be used to find the combination of inputs and outputs that would maximize the firm's profits.

For the crops and farming operations in the analysis reported here, mathematical programming was used to determine the combination of crops and outputs that maximize the sum of farmers' profits plus the consumer's surplus obtained by solutions of the problem—first, under the assumption that there is *no air pollution* and, second, under the assumption that the levels of air pollution (ozone) prevailing in 1976 were in effect.

The difference between consumer's surplus plus profit under the two circumstances is, then, an estimate of the ecomomic damage, or inversely, of the benefits of cleaning up from a condition of 1976 pollution to no pollution at all. The needed information about the links between air pollution and yield and about demand elasticities for various crops were both obtained from the literature which exists in southern California on these matters, and through original statistical analyses by the researchers. The concept of consumer's surplus plus producer's profit is left at an intuitive level here. The methodology used for the discussion of ozone damage later in this chapter lends itself more readily to graphic depiction, and a geometric interpretation of the benefit concept used here is given there.

For the regions analyzed, table 9-1 presents estimated air pollution-induced, percentage-yield reductions for 1976 for the fourteen crops studied, given the actual 1976 cropping patterns and locations. Four vegetable crops—broccoli, cantaloupes, carrots, and cauliflower—displayed no yield effects in these estimates. Reductions in lettuce yields occured only in the South Coast, and these effects were slight. However, lima beans, celery, and cotton suffered substantial yield reductions, while potatoes, tomatoes, and onions exhibited moderate losses at observed pollution levels. Regional percentage-yield reductions were by far the greatest in the South Coast, followed by the southern San Joaquin, the

Table 9-1. Air-Pollution Effect on Percentage-Yield Reductions for Selected Regions in 1976

Crop	Percentage reduction in yield associated with increase in ozone from zero to 1976 level			
	Southern Desert	South Coast	Central Coast	Southern San Joaquin
Vegetables				
Beans, and processing				
green lima	—	15.71	1.57	9.45
Broccoli	—	0.00	0.00	—
Cantaloupes	0.00	0.00	n.a.	0.00
Carrots	0.00	0.00	0.00	0.00
Cauliflower	—	0.00	0.00	—
Celery	—	12.57	1.23	—
Lettuce, head	0.00	0.03	0.00	0.00
Onions, fresh	0.00	1.99	0.40	—
Onions, processing	0.00	1.99	0.40	1.35
Potatoes	—	4.20	4.30	1.95
Tomatoes, fresh	0.00	4.20	0.43	1.95
Tomatoes, processing	0.00	4.20	0.43	1.95
Field				
Cotton	9.40	18.70	n.a.	6.90
Sugar beets	0.00	1.63	0.33	1.10

Note: Dashes indicate no production of that crop in that region. Zeros indicate no change in production (due to the insignificant effect of air pollution on that crop); and n.a. indicates data are not available.

Source: Based on data from Richard M. Adams, Narongsakdi Thanivibulchai, and Thomas D. Crocker, *A Preliminary Assessment of Air Pollution Damages for Assessing Air Pollution Damages for Selected Crops Within Southern California,* vol. 3 of *Methods Development for Assessing Air Pollution Control Benefits,* EPA-600-5-001C (Washington, D.C., EPA, 1979) p. 82.

Southern Desert, and the Central Coast regions. This ordering of regions by yield reductions corresponds to how they rate in terms of smog conditions.

To estimate the extent to which air pollution reduced crop production in the individual study regions, the 1976 percentage-yield reductions were used to calculate what per-acre yields for each crop in each region would have been if there had been no air pollution. Given these new per-acre yields, the mathematical programming model was used to calculate new cropping patterns and locations of production, as well as associated effects on producer profits and consumer surplus.

The results show that the Southern Desert region would experience a slight increase in production of most crops susceptible to air pollution damages, with significant increases in the production of processing onions and cotton. Those crops more resistant to air-pollution damages, such as carrots and lettuce, exhibit slight declines in production.

For the other three regions, some crops, such as cauliflower, lettuce, and broccoli, that are somewhat tolerant of air pollution, record minimal changes in production levels. However, broccoli and cantaloupes in the South Coast region are exceptions to this. The very significant decrease in the production of these pollution-tolerant crops stems from their substantially reduced profitability relative to crops that are more sensitive to air pollution. Production of those pollution-sensitive crops, such as lima beans, potatoes, tomatoes, cotton, and onions, generally tends to increase in each region. As would be expected, since 1976 air-pollution levels were relatively small, only minimal changes in crop production occurred in the Central Coast region.

Let us now turn to the central objective of the analysis—estimated differences in the value of consumer surplus plus profit "with" and "without" 1976 levels of air pollution, and the distribution of these differences among producers and consumers. Table 9-2 gives this information for all the regions combined.

The results indicate that elimination of oxidant air pollution and attendant net increases in aggregate production would have increased 1976 producer profits by about $35 million and consumer surpluses by about $10 million, resulting in an increase of about $45 million in the

Table 9-2. Economic Value of Air-Pollution Crop Damage in Southern California

	Total consumer surplus plus producer profit ($)	Producer profits ($)	Consumer surplus ($)
With air pollution effects	1,447,733,227	1,086,788,371	370,944,856
Without air pollution effects	1,503,024,714	1,122,024,497	381,000,217
Estimated losses due to air pollution	45,291,487	35,236,126	10,055,361

Source: Based on data from Richard M. Adams, Narongsakdi Thanivibulchai, and Thomas D. Crocker, A Preliminary Assessment of Air Pollution Damages for Assessing Air Pollution Damages for Selected Crops Within Southern California, vol. 3 of Methods Development for Assessing Air Pollution Control Benefits, EPA-600-5-001C (Washington, D.C., EPA, 1979) p. 82.

total. This latter figure represents a little under 4 percent of the $1.22 billion total farm value of the fourteen crops produced in the four regions in 1976. About $30 million of the estimated potential increase in the total is due to an improvement in cotton yields. While this is a significant amount, accepting the results in chapter 6, it is outweighed by urban damages in the same region by at least a factor of ten. This result for the most severely polluted, major agricultural region in the country and for the assumption that *all* pollution is eliminated (probably an impossibility and certainly uneconomical) suggests the possibility that the economic costs of air pollution in the agricultural sector are also relatively small in the rest of the United States.

That this is incorrect will be shown in the section which follows. There, ozone damage to field crops across the nation as a whole is assessed by the use of a procedure designed especially for that purpose. The reason for this result is that the total value of major crops like wheat, corn, cotton, and peanuts is so enormous that even relatively small reductions in yield can cause large economic losses for the nation as a whole.

Ozone Damage to U.S. Agriculture

The study described in the previous section is a detailed look at pollution damage in a single, but very important, agricultural region in the United States. The researchers were able to incorporate adjustments to pollution—for example, crop switching—in considerable detail. In principle, this approach could be applied, region by region, to the entire country. But the resources required to do so would be considerable and well beyond those available for the project described here.

Therefore, in the interest of estimating national agricultural benefits, it was necessary to develop a simpler methodology, one that could use existing data sets. Data limitations laid some restrictions on the study. The only pollutant considered was ozone, and the only crops considered were wheat, corn, cotton, soybeans, and peanuts. But ozone is thought to be the major pollutant affecting agriculture, and these five field crops

AUTHOR'S NOTE: This section is based primarily on Raymond J. Kopp, William J. Vaughan, and Michael Hazilla, "Agricultural Benefits Analysis for Ozone: Methods Evaluation and Demonstration," Final Report prepared for the U.S. Environmental Protection Agency, Office of Air Quality Planning and Standards (Research Triangle Park, N.C., EPA, 1983).

account for more than 60 percent of the total value of U.S. agricultural production.

The methodology developed to assess agricultural damage on a national scale is called the Region Model Farm (RMF) approach. Essential to this approach is a set of data developed and maintained by the U.S. Department of Agriculture (USDA). The USDA refers to these data as the Firm Enterprise Data System (FEDS). The FEDS provides those studying agriculture with sample operating budgets that describe the entire cost structure for producing an acre of a particular crop in a specific region of the continental United States. The budget is representative of the average agricultural practice in that region and is verified with a battery of farm-level surveys every two years. A single budget for the production of soybeans in southeastern North Carolina, for example, may include cost information on as many as 200 inputs to agricultural production, the average yield per acre to be expected, and the total number of acres planted in the region. FEDS divides the United States into more than 200 producing areas. Thus, when the present study examines the cost of producing wheat, for example, it considers production cost for more than 160 regions where wheat is produced in the United States.

The reason why this fine detail on costs is needed is that the major way in which pollution affects agriculture is through yield reduction. Since this is so, reduction of pollution will permit a particular amount of agricultural production to take place at reduced cost. This cost reduction is one, and the largest, component of benefits (reduced damage) of pollution control. Thus, if one can calculate this reduction on a national scale, a major step will have been taken in estimating agricultural benefits. To do this, total costs of agricultural production must be calculated before and after pollution control, and since costs of production vary by region, the fine regional detail provided by FEDS is needed to do this accurately.

To calculate cost, the researchers assumed that for each of the FEDS producing areas, the representative farm budget for a particular crop type reflects both the cost and yield existing for that budget year, for given prices of inputs, outputs, and ambient ozone concentrations. The FEDS budgets are on a per-acre basis and can be added up across all of the planted acres covered by a budget for a particular crop.

Given these data, the aggregate cost of production can be estimated for whatever the actual output is in a given year. The procedure used assumes that production is limited by available land for a particular crop in a given region. All the regions capable of producing the crop under consideration are then arrayed in order of increasing cost for the entire country under the further assumption that each region produces the maximum output that available land will allow. This assumption will be true for all regions except the highest-cost region included, where the maximum output may not be needed to complete the total output actually produced in a particular year, say, 1982.

One can show how this works with the aid of a simple illustration that shows the results of this procedure for only the least-cost region, say, for corn, and for the next higher one (figure 9-2).

As shown, the total cost of producing corn in the lowest-cost region is the unit cost times the amount produced there and, similarly, for the next lowest cost region, and so on, until the quantity produced equals the actual national output for that year. Since there are up to 160 regions that could produce a particular crop, a graph such as figure 9-2, but including all regions, would closely resemble a smooth curve when seen as a whole (see figure 9-3).

To economists, such a curve is known as a *marginal cost curve*. It displays the *increment* in total cost for each unit as output is increased. Paralleling the principles discussed in chapter 2 with respect to demand concepts, the area under a marginal cost curve equals the total cost of producing whatever number of units of output are produced.

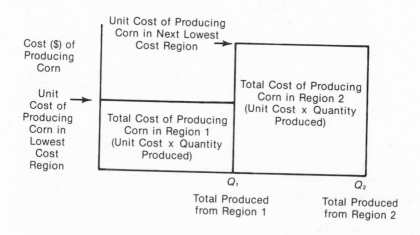

Figure 9-2.

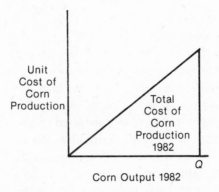

Figure 9-3.

How are these ideas related to estimating the benefits from reduced ozone? As stated, the major source of benefits (reduced damages) comes from the ability to produce any specified output at lower cost when pollution effects are controlled. The effect of this is to shift the marginal cost curve downward (figure 9-4).

The difference between the areas under the two curves, area *B*, would then be the benefit of reducing pollution to such an extent that marginal production costs would fall to the lower curve, for the moment taking output as given.

We have seen how the upper curve can be calculated with existing data, but how do we get to the lower curve? To do so, further information is needed: (1) one must know the ozone level of each producing area; (2) one must know how a proposed ozone policy would affect each of these

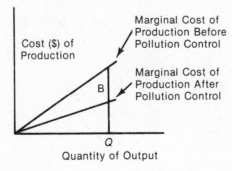

Figure 9-4.

levels; and (3) one must know how this change in level would affect yield (the dose-response relationship we have encountered so frequently).

The first two items were supplied by EPA specialists based on extrapolations from ozone-monitoring stations and on estimated effects of possible pollution-control policies. The third item was estimated by the research team from another data set available from the EPA. These data result from experimental work conducted by the National Crop Loss Assessment Network or NCLAN. Particular crop varieties are subjected to alternate levels of ozone under laboratory conditions of experimental control. The relationship between yield and ozone concentrations for each crop is then estimated from these data by statistical regression—the technique we have encountered often before.

With these items of information at hand, it is a straightforward matter to estimate a marginal cost curve corresponding to a new level of ozone concentration.

But as previously indicated, if costs are significantly affected by pollution, a price change will occur, and an associated change in consumer surplus will take place. Thus, to get a complete estimate of benefits, one must calculate the change in consumer surplus as well as the cost change.

If the demand curve is as shown in figure 9-5, price would fall from P_1 (under the original cost conditions) to P_2 (under the new cost conditions). In an industry where there is no significant element of monopoly, price is determined by the intersection of the marginal cost line and the demand line. This is because at any price above this, consumers are willing to pay more than it costs to produce additional units of output, and at any lower price, additional units of output cannot be sold for what it costs to produce them.

In figure 9-5, the area oxy is the reduction in cost discussed in connection with figure 9-4. But the area xyz is an *additional* benefit which, in accordance with principles discussed earlier, consists of increases

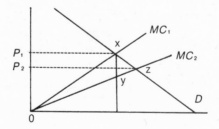

Figure 9-5.

in both consumer surplus and producer profit. When this area is included, the benefit measure used is conceptually the same as the benefit measure used previously. To estimate this additional benefit quantitatively, one must have an estimate of the elasticity of demand for each crop. For purposes of the study described here, these estimates were taken from the published literature.

Using these tools, estimates of benefits were made for two different regimes of ozone change. The first, specified by EPA, must be regarded as highly unrealistic. The second, developed by the research team, seems more plausible.

Under the EPA scenario, it is assumed that for any hypothetical ozone standard which is to be evaluated, all rural areas will be exactly at that standard. Since particular areas currently may be either above or below that standard, under the EPA scenario gains and losses may cancel each other out. It is even possible that change from the existing situation to a tighter standard, given the uniformity assumption, could result in negative benefits. Since ozone stems mainly from urban areas, it seems more realistic to assume that if the standard is tightened in those areas, levels would also fall in the affected rural areas and not rise anywhere else. The scenarios developed by the research staff make this assumption.

Also note that very few ozone monitors exist in rural areas. Thus, the estimates for those areas usually are extrapolated from measurements made in the nearest urban areas. The accuracy of these extrapolations is very uncertain, thus adding to the uncertainties inherent in other parts of the estimating procedure.

Interestingly, even under the EPA scenario, a substantial reduction in ozone concentrations is calculated to yield large benefits. For example, in the southeastern United States—the largest soybean-producing region in the nation—the average rural ambient ozone concentration was estimated to be about .055 parts per million (ppm) in 1978. The concentration at urban monitors is usually about twice that estimated for rural areas, or in this case, about .11 or .12 ppm. The current national ambient standard is .12 ppm. According to the model calculation, a standard of .05 ppm, if that concentration prevailed everywhere in rural areas in the region, would yield benefits in soybean production of more than $600 million. An extreme reduction to .01 ppm would yield benefits of more than $2 billion in that region alone, according to the model, but such a large reduction is probably impossible to achieve.

As noted, benefits also were calculated on the basis of more realistic assumptions about what would happen to ozone levels in rural areas after the urban ozone standard is tightened—namely, that concentrations in rural areas would also go down. It was assumed that alternative ambient standards would apply at sites where ozone is actually monitored. The translation of that standard into ambient levels in rural areas was then accomplished by means of a very simple dispersion model (see chapter 3). Otherwise, the methodology was the same as that described previously and used to estimate the EPA scenarios. Table 9-3 gives some of the results. It was assumed that the national ambient standard of .12 ppm was met initially at each monitoring site. This is the base for the calculation of benefits associated with increasingly strict hypothetical standards. The values in table 9-3 are in 1978 dollars and represent total national benefits for each of the crops listed.

Table 9-3 shows large national benefits from comparatively small reductions in ozone concentrations. This is because, even though effects on yields may not be especially large, the total value of annual production of these crops is so enormous that even a small yield response translates into a large number of dollars of benefits. For example, the total national production (price times quantity) of soybeans has in recent years been in the $12 to $14 billion range.

As usual, uncertainties pertain to these results. But they do suggest that agricultural benefits of ozone control could be quite large.

Table 9-3. Effect of Reduced Ozone Concentrations on Production of Selected Crops

Ozone concentration (ppm)	Peanuts	Cotton	Corn	Wheat	Soybeans
.09	60,340,144	224,475,376	89,470,640	111,910,464	528,989,790
.10	46,293,184	154,554,480	69,072,704	78,979,552	391,863,126
.11	24,786,876	73,884,528	37,716,928	37,963,072	203,381,141
.12	0	0	0	0	0

Source: Data from Raymond J. Kopp, William J. Vaughan, and Michael Hazilla, "Agricultural Sector Benefits Analysis for Ozone: Methods Evaluation and Demonstration" (Research Triangle Park, N.C., U.S. Environmental Protection Agency, Office of Air Quality Planning and Standards, 1983).

10

NATIONAL FRESHWATER BENEFITS OF WATER-POLLUTION CONTROL

This chapter presents two studies that endeavor to develop methods for assessing the *national* benefits associated with improvements in, or maintenance of, the quality of surface waters. The first focuses exclusively on freshwater fishing and builds up a national total from regional estimates. The second uses a national sample survey technique to elicit individual's valuation of some broad national water-quality goals.

National Freshwater Recreation Benefits

Among the more important pieces of national environmental legislation created during the 1970s were the comprehensive amendments to the Federal Water Pollution Control Act. These amendments, signed into law in 1972 and further amended in 1977, in reality constituted a major piece of legislation in their own right, dramatically redirecting the nation's efforts at water-pollution control and setting out ambitious national goals, expressed both in terms of discharge controls and of resulting water quality.

AUTHOR'S NOTE: This section is based primarily on William J. Vaughan and Clifford S. Russell, *Freshwater Recreational Fishing: The National Benefits of Water Pollution Control* (Washington, D.C., Resources for the Future, 1982).

Criticism of the amendments and debate over their goals and requirements began during the legislative process and has continued, with more
or less heat, to the present. Some critics argue that the goals are too
ambitious, that is, the benefits of meeting the goals (and related
requirements) are thought to be too small to justify the costs of compliance.
This argument over the balance of benefits and costs can never be resolved
entirely by research, but the RFF project described here was undertaken
in the conviction that it should be possible to improve methods for
estimating at least some of the benefit categories associated with water-
pollution control, in this case, the benefits from recreational fishing in
U.S. freshwater bodies. From the outset the intent was to design a
method for estimating benefits for the nation as a whole rather than
benefits for particular sites. In this respect, it resembles the study
discussed in the last part of chapter 9.

In undertaking this project, a primary question concerned the ways in
which water-quality improvement would favorably affect freshwater
fishing. Two major ways were identified.

First, it tends to increase the total availability of fishable freshwater
bodies by reducing the incidence of conditions such as low dissolved
oxygen that results from the bacterial degradation of organic materials
and heavy sediment loads that make it difficult for fish to survive.

Second, it produces changes in the *types* of fish that can survive in
particular water bodies.

Simply put, clean water means "game" fish such as trout or bass, and
dirty water means rough fish such as carp or buffalo. In general, fishermen
prefer game fish. Therefore, pollution control tends to increase the amount
of water yielding high-quality fishing relative to that yielding low-quality
fishing.

Given this view of the benefit-producing mechanisms, one can work
toward a methodology for making national benefit estimates based on it.
As explained in chapters 3 and 4, benefit estimation for environmental
improvement requires the understanding of a number of links. For this
particular study, the following questions should be considered:

1. How will implementation of the law affect pollution discharges by
   location, quantity, and pollutant type across the entire nation?
2. How will the pre- and postpolicy discharge levels affect ambient
   water quality? Or how does ambient quality change as discharges

change not only in terms of such familiar indicators as dissolved oxygen, but also in terms of supportable fish population types?

3. How will increases in total amounts of water supporting recreational fishing and shifts in the composition of that water toward more highly valued fish species affect the number of anglers and the amount of time they spend fishing?

4. In addition, one needs to be able to value fishing activity of various kinds—that is, for practical purposes, how many days are spent fishing for various species—rough fish versus game fish?

The novelty of this study and its main contribution to methodological development lies in the ingenious way it is able to link models together to structure these linkages and how it is able to take existing and newly developed data sets to estimate them quantitatively. I turn now to a discussion of each step in the procedure.

Discharge Reductions and Links to Ambient Quality and Fish

Initially, one must have an understanding of the "fishability" of the nation's water prior to the implementation of the Federal Water Pollution Control Act. A data base is available from the Fish and Wildlife Service that permits estimates of fishable water by state (the state is the basic geographic unit on which this study is operated), but these data do not provide a basis for the breakdown between rough fish and game fish that is basic to the methods used in this study. For this reason, the researchers surveyed state fish-and-game officials asking them for a breakdown by species category within their own states. Using these data, they found that for the contiguous forty-eight states and the District of Columbia, there are about 30.6 million acres of fishable fresh water consisting of about 20.4 percent cold-water game fisheries, 68.4 percent warm-water game fisheries, and 11.2 percent rough fisheries.

To determine how the implementation of discharge controls would affect the current status requires a knowledge of the amount and location of discharges prior to, and following, the implementation of the 1972 amendments. Then it is necessary to estimate how this change will affect ambient conditions in water courses, and how, in turn, these will affect fishability.

The first three kinds of information have been established by the use of RFF's Water Quality Network (WQN) model (see chapter 3). This model, designed specifically to answer those questions, was run for four scenarios representing—albeit roughly in some cases—stages in the implementation of the law. In what follows, I will focus on only one of these stages—the Best Practical Control Technology Currently Available. This is for simplicity and also because the quantitative benefits still must be regarded as experimental. The Best Practical Control Technology Currently Available (BPT for short) requirement was to be achieved by all point sources (that is, discharges from confined channels, such as pipes) of wastewater discharge by July 1, 1977. This unmet goal may reflect where we currently are in our control efforts.

At best, the WQN model provides a reasonable estimate of the impact of policy changes on one important aspect of ambient conditions: dissolved oxygen. However, it does not translate directly into fishability. Indeed, making that step is an undeveloped discipline, calling for heroic measures. Fortunately, a fisheries biologist, willing to use his knowledge and skill to survey the literature, developed a set of rules that appear to capture whatever consensus exists on the water-quality conditions appropriate to the survival and reproduction of various fish populations. These rules can be applied to the results of the WQN model to provide estimates of the acreages of different kinds of fishing availability by state, and by aggregation, for the nation as a whole. The results for BPT for the whole country are shown in table 10-1.

The reader may be struck by how small the increases in total fishable

Table 10-1. Percentage Changes in Fishery Shares from Baseline Situation

	Total fishable water (in thousands acres)	Baseline and projected		
		Fishery shares (%)		
		Cold-water gamefish	Warm-water gamefish-panfish	Rough fish
Pre-Federal Water Pollution Control Act–Clean Water Act conditions	30,615	20.4	68.4	11.2
Pollution control to level represented by BPT	30,721	22.7	73.6	3.7

Source: Based on data from William J. Vaughan and Clifford S. Russell, *Freshwater Recreational Fishing: The National Benefits of Water Pollution Control* (Washington, D.C., Resources for the Future, 1982), table 2-9, p. 54.

water are—only about 100,000 acres from a base of more than 30 million. This is because a very large proportion of U.S. fresh waters already was fishable before implementation of the water-pollution law. However, at the same time, it is projected that the waters regarded as unfishable or capable of supporting rough fish only will decline dramatically. This does not mean a proportionate decline in rough fish populations, but rather a large increase in the water that rough fish will share with warm- and cold-water game fish.

The next step is to devise ways of converting the water-quality results into changes in fishermen's participation in various kinds of fishing. Before proceeding, however, it is pertinent to note that what has been discussed so far is not types of research and modeling that are in the usual purview of economics. But the situation here, as in other chapters, is reflective of the fact that existing models of natural systems rarely fit the needs of the economist who would estimate the benefits of environmental improvement. Accordingly, he is often forced into disciplinary imperialism.

Behavioral Economic Aspects of the Study

I now turn to steps in the analysis that are more clearly economic in character. In order to estimate total activity in various types of fishing, the individual fisherman's chain of decision about recreational fishing must be broken down into several logical stages.

The first choice is whether to do any fishing at all. The researchers' hypothesis is that the decision of whether to fish is sensitive, among other things, to the opportunity to fish, represented by the quantity of fishable water. The object of this first stage of the research is then to quantitatively estimate how the decision to fish is influenced, in the population at large, by the availability of fishable water. Regression analysis is the method used to determine the separate influences of availability of fishing opportunity and those other factors that might affect the decision (for example, income or sex of respondent).

The indicators of existing availability of fishable water are the state-level estimates divided by the state population to get a per capita measure. This is rather crude, but a more refined indicator was not available at the time.

The other data needed for this stage of the research were obtained from a very large survey conducted by the U.S. Department of the

Interior, Fish and Wildlife Service in 1975. The first or screening stage of this survey was conducted by telephone interview of more than 100,000 households (300,000 individuals). Its primary intent was to determine whether individuals participated in hunting, fishing, and other recreational activities associated with wildlife. The survey also contained information on other pertinent variables such as age, sex, income, and other factors so that it was possible to include them in the regression analysis and control for their possible effects on participation. The dependent variable was the decision to fish or not to fish. Since the availability of fishable water was included among the independent variables, once the coefficients of the equation have been estimated, the size of the availability variable can be changed and the corresponding change in participation calculated. We have seen regression analysis results used in a similar way in other chapters, for example, in projecting the effect of air-quality improvement (see chapter 8).

So far, all the analysis permits us to do is to project fishing in general as a function of water quality. But since, as I have indicated, different types of fishing (warm-water game fishing, cold-water game fishing, and rough fishing) probably differ in value, we must also be able to project how likely a representative individual is to pick each of these types if he or she does decide to fish.

For this purpose, data obtained by the Fish and Wildlife Service in the second stage of the 1975 survey was used. A questionnaire was mailed to more than 50,000 persons who had declared themselves to be hunters or fishermen in the screening stage. For this subgroup, detailed information was gathered on their participation patterns, socioeconomic characteristics, and preferences. Data for the fishermen only was used in analyzing the second stage in the decision chain—namely, once a person has decided to fish how likely is he or she to participate in each of the three types of fishing given the availability of water suitable for each type? Because doing some trout fishing, for example, does not rule out doing some bass or rough fishing as well during the course of the year, the regression equations for the type of fishing decision might best be characterized in "some-of" terms. Either a person did some cold-water game fishing or he or she did not. But the individual also might have done some bass fishing. In any case, whether some of a particular kind of fishing was done was hypothesized to be a function of the availability of water suitable for that kind of fishing as well as other characteristics of the participant.

The final stage in the decision chain is the decision on how much time (how many days) will be spent in that activity. The same set of survey data was used in the analysis of this question, and regression analysis was the tool for connecting reported decisions on days of fishing to the independent variables, including the availability of water suitable for the fishing in question.

The drift of the analysis is now clear. The steps are as follows: the amount of increase in total fishable water and fishable-type water associated with water-pollution control is given for the nation as a whole from the models of the previous sections. Given this, the results of Stage 1 are used to calculate how much fishing participation will increase in general. Then, the results of Stages 2 and 3 are used to calculate how this increase in participation will be distributed across the fishing types and how many days of increased fishing of each type will occur nationally as a result of the pollution-control policy. This process and some results are laid out in table 10-2.

Table 10-2. Summary of Results for Participation Changes

Results of survey	Water quality	
	Base	After BPT
Probability of being a fisherman	0.2793	0.2794
Total fisherman (10^6)	59.16	59.18
Probability of doing some fishing		
Cold-water gamefish fishing	0.3708	0.3931
Warm-water gamefish fishing	0.6840	0.6776
Rough fishing	0.3499	0.3536
Days per angler per year of		
Cold-water gamefish fishing	13.76	13.73
Warm-water gamefish fishing	18.22	18.49
Rough fishing	10.14	10.55
Total days per year of		
Cold-water gamefish fishing (10^6)	301.8	319.3
Warm-water gamefish fishing (10^6)	737.4	741.4
Rough fishing (10^6)	209.8	220.8

Source: Based on data from William J. Vaughan and Clifford S. Russell, Freshwater Recreational Fishing: The National Benefits of Water Pollution Control (Washington, D.C., Resources for the Future, 1982), table 6-1, p. 156.

The final problem confronted by this research on the benefits from improved freshwater fishing opportunities is how to assign dollar-value benefits (that is, willingness to pay) to the increase in each category of fishing activity. The approach adopted estimated a demand curve for fishing days for each category and used those to calculate the average consumer's surplus per day. The travel-cost method, described generally in chapter 2, was the technique selected. I now turn to a brief discussion of how it was applied in this study.

Recall that the basic assumption of the travel-cost method is that higher costs of access, as reflected in distance from a recreational site, will have the same effect on visitation as an equivalent admission fee assuming zero distance from the site. In chapter 4, I presented a very simple example of how this relationship can be used to develop a demand curve by assuming successively higher admissions fees and using information on access costs to estimate their effects on visitation. This establishes points on a demand curve, that is, the relationship of price to the number of visitor-days. The area under the demand curve, by principles discussed in chapter 2, is the total willingness to pay of participants for the total number of visitor-days to the site, say, a trout fishery. If one then divides the number of visitor-days into this number, one obtains the average willingness to pay for a day of fishing for trout. The researchers who conducted the study collected data from a large number of fishing sites around the country which permitted them, by statistical means, to make exactly such a calculation yielding average willingness to pay per visitor-day for each type of fishery.

Estimating National Water-Quality Benefits

We are now at a point where a national benefits estimate can be made. All the earlier machinations were designed to estimate how many days of increased recreational fishing of each type would correspond to the water-quality changes resulting from a reduction of wastewater discharges corresponding to the implementation of a pollution-control policy. Having these numbers in hand, it is a simple matter to multiply them by average willingness to pay for a day by fish type and get a total benefit number for freshwater fishing in the United States. When this is done, the following results are obtained for Best Practical Control Technology Currently Available.

Valuation base	Total annual benefits over base (millions of 1980$)
Low	307
High	683

A few words of explanation are needed about the difference between the low and the high estimates. For the low estimate, travel cost is based only on out-of-pocket expenses—gasoline, restaurant food, motels, and others. This is the conventional method. The higher estimate takes account of the fact that the fisherman may also attach a cost to the time it takes to get to the site. For the higher figure, an estimate of this cost is made by attaching average wage rates to the travel time needed to reach the site.

Needless to say, large uncertainties attend these numbers and, because of this, they must be regarded as largely experimental. Nevertheless, in view of the heavy costs of the national program for water-quality improvement they may strike the reader as being quite low. There are several things to be said in this connection. First, the reader should recall that in terms of the availability of fish species the vast majority of the nation's fresh water was already fishable prior to the 1972 Amendments. Second, these estimates are partial in the sense that they consider only the fresh waters of the United States, and even then they do not include values that may accrue to fishermen from the possible effects of pollution control on the aesthetic aspects of the fishing experience.

At present, research is under way to extend the methodology developed in this study to effects of pollution control on marine (saltwater) recreational fisheries, and on both marine and freshwater swimming and recreational boating.

A Survey Method for Estimating National Water-Quality Benefits

The research reported in the previous section was designed to yield national recreational fishing benefits of water-quality improvement.

AUTHOR'S NOTE: This section is based primarily on Robert Cameron Mitchell and Richard T. Carson, "An Experiment in Measuring Willingness to Pay for Intrinsic Water Pollution Control Benefits," A Report to the U.S. Environmental Protection Agency (Washington, D.C., Resources for the Future, 1981).

Basically, it used subregions as units of analysis and aggregated them by adding up the results. In this sense it is still "site specific," although less so than, say, the visibility study reported in chapter 11. Thus it can be described as a large-scale simulation falling somewhere between a particular site (or micro) study and a national survey that asks respondents directly about their willingness to pay for *national* programs of pollution control. This last procedure has been called the "macro" approach. Among other potential advantages of such an approach, two are especially important. First, a randomized national sample of persons can be interviewed which permits the use of well-established statistical procedures to extrapolate the results to the entire population. Second, one can inquire about "intrinsic" or existence benefits as well as user benefits.

The second reason invites more explanation. Because the U.S. population politically supports very expensive programs of water-pollution conrol—much more costly than the benefits estimated for recreational users in the previous section—the researchers were led to believe that there must be some form or forms of benefits accruing to persons who do not actually use particular water bodies. We have termed such benefits variously as intrinsic or existence benefits. These benefits may accrue because persons value the options for possible use that are opened to them when water bodies are cleaned up. This type of value, discussed widely in the economics literature, has come to be called the option value. Other intrinsic values may accrue from a sense of national pride or rectitude associated with having clean waters. One of the main conclusions of the research reported in this chapter and in the following one is that intrinsic benefits definitely exist with respect to environmental improvements or maintenance. Moreover, and with the usual caution about accuracy of results, not only do they exist, but they are large, perhaps even larger than user benefits in some instances.

Some aspects of water quality make it more appropriate than air quality for an experimental application of the macro approach. Chiefly, goals of our national policy are set out in a manner that would let most of the population understand what they mean in terms of ordinary experience. The objectives are to make all the nation's water fishable and swimmable in successive stages. Furthermore, much of the cost of these programs is to be paid from taxes levied at the national levels (taxes financing subsidies to local governments) so that respondents can be realistically asked how much in added tax burden they are willing to pay for improved water quality across the whole nation. Neither one of these situations holds with respect to air quality, so it would be much harder to pose understandable and realistic alternatives in a national clean air survey.

A macro study, then, is potentially useful for doing a benefit–cost analysis for national water programs. It should be noted, however, that it is *not* a substitute for site-specific studies in other applications. For example, determining whether the benefits outweigh the costs of a program for water-quality improvement in the Potomac estuary would require a site-specific study.

Research Procedures

One problem with national surveys is that they are quite expensive. What made it possible to conduct an experiment with the macro approach, given available resources, was that the researchers were able to add some water-quality questions onto a survey being funded by another source. After the interview for the other survey was completed, the interviewers administered a sequence of benefits questions that had been carefully pretested by researchers on the benefits project. From the respondents' perspective, the two interviews appeared as one long interview. In all, 1,576 personal interviews of a national probability sample of persons eighteen years of age and older were completed. The sample was designed and the interviews were conducted by Roper and Cantril, a national polling firm.

A penalty of this add-on approach proved to be that an unfortunately large number of persons failed to complete all of the questions. In part this was because they came at the end of an already fairly lengthy survey and in part because it was not possible to undertake special training of the interviewers to administer the benefits section. Because of the likelihood of item-response bias (caused by respondents failing to answer individual items), the researchers regard their estimates as only suggestive and warn against accepting them as definitive. The main intent of the experiment was not to develop definitive estimates at this stage but to test whether a macro approach is applicable to an investigation of water-quality benefits.

The low response rate presumably can be cured by an improved questionnaire and by training of the interviewers. A study is currently being planned in which both of these elements will exist.

The Water-Pollution Ladder and Value Levels

The levels of water quality for which the research team sought willingness-to-pay estimates are "boatable," "fishable," and "swimmable." These levels are described in words and depicted graphically by means of a "water-quality ladder" (figure 10-1). Use of these categories, two of which are embodied in the law mandating the national program for water-pollution control, permitted avoidance of the communications problems associated with describing water quality in terms of the numerous

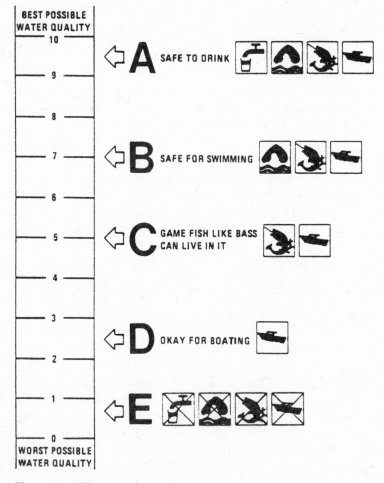

Figure 10-1. Water-quality ladder card.

abstract technical measures of pollution (oxygen depletion, for example). Although the boatable–fishable–swimmable categories are widely understood by the public, they did require further specification to ensure that different people perceived them in a similar fashion.

Boatable water was defined as an intermediate level between water which "has oil, raw sewage and other things in it, has no plant or animal life and smells bad" on the one hand, and water which is of fishable quality on the other. As discussed earlier, *fishable water* covers a fairly large range of water quality. Game fish such as bass and trout cannot tolerate water in which certain rough fish such as carp and catfish flourish. In pretests, experiments were made with two levels of fishable water— one for rough fish like carp and catfish, and the other for game fish like bass—but a single definition of fishable was adopted as water "clean enough so that game fish like bass can live in it," under the assumption that the words "game fish" and "bass" had wide recognition and denoted water of the quality that Congress had in mind. *Swimmable water* appeared to present less difficulty for popular understanding since the enforcement of water-quality standards for swimming by health authorities has led to widespread awareness that swimming in polluted water can cause illness.

Because willingness-to-pay questions have to describe in some detail the conditions of the "market" for the good, they are inevitably longer than the usual survey research questions. Respondents quickly become bored and restless if material is read to them without giving them frequent opportunities to express judgments or to look at visual aids. The questionnaire for this experiment was designed to be as interactive as possible by interpreting the text with questions which required the respondents to use the newly described water-quality categories. They were also handed a card depicting the water-quality ladder which was referred to constantly during the sequence of benefits questions.

Figure 10-1 shows the card. The top, step 10, was called the "best possible water quality," and the bottom, step 0, was the "worst possible water quality." The card is "anchored" by designating five levels of water quality at different steps on the ladder. Level E, at 0.8, was specified as a point on the ladder where the water was unfit even for boating. Level D, 2.5, was where it became safe for boating; level C, at 5, was fishable; level B, at 7, was swimmable; and 9.5 was identified as level A, where the water is safe to drink.

Willingness-to-Pay Questions and Answers

Questions about willingness to pay should seem realistic to respondents. Accordingly, they were couched in terms of annual household payments in higher prices and taxes because this is the way people do pay for water-pollution control. A portion of each household's annual federal tax payment goes toward the expense of regulating water pollution and providing construction grants for sewage-treatment plants. Local sewage taxes pay for the maintenance of these plants. Those private users, such as manufacturing plants, who incur pollution-control expenses ultimately pass much or all of the cost along to consumers in higher prices. Thus, this payment method has a ring of truth to the respondents.

As explained in chapter 4, "starting-point bias" can be an important problem in bidding games and surveys. That is, a high starting bid from an interviewer may elicit a higher bid from a respondent than a low starting bid. A major methodological innovation of the research reported in this chapter is the development of a device for eliminating such a bias, the "payment card."

In this technique, the respondent is given a card which contains a menu of alternative amounts of payment beginning at $0 and increasing by a fixed interval until an arbitrarily determined large amount is reached. When the time comes to elicit the amount one is willing to pay, the respondent is asked to pick a number from the card (or any number in between) which "is the *most* you would be willing to pay in taxes and higher price *each year*" (italics in the questionnaire) for a given level of water quality. Thus, the interviewer suggests no bid at all.

It turns out, however, that this presents some problems of its own. In initial pretests, it was found that the respondents had considerable difficulty in determining their willingness to pay when a card was used which only presented various dollar amounts. A number of them expressed embarrassment, confusion, or resentment at the task, and some who gave amounts indicated they were very uncertain about them. The problem lay with the lack of benchmarks for their estimates. People are not normally aware of the total amounts they pay for public goods even when that amount comes out of their taxes, nor do they know how much such goods cost. Without a way of psychologically anchoring their estimate in some manner, they were not able to arrive at meaningful estimates. They needed benchmarks of some kind which would convey sufficient information without biasing their responses. Their most appropriate benchmarks for willingness to pay for water-pollution control would appear to be the amounts they are already paying in higher prices and taxes for other nonenvironmental, publicly provided goods and services. Amounts were identified on the card for several such goods, and further pretests were conducted, indicating that the benchmarks made the task meaningful for most people.

But the use of payment cards with benchmarks raises the possibility of introducing its own kind of bias. Are the respondents who gave amounts for water-pollution control using the benchmarks for general orientation or are they basing their amounts directly on the benchmarks themselves in some manner? In the former case, respondents would be giving unique values for water quality; in the latter case, they would be giving values for water quality relative to what they think they are paying for a particular set of other public goods. If the latter case holds and their water-quality values are sensitive to changes in the benchmark amounts, or to changes in the set of public goods identified on the payment card, their validity as estimates of consumer surplus for water quality are suspect. A test for this kind of bias was conducted in the pretest by using different versions of the payment card with the amounts paid for other publicly provided goods changed by modest amounts. No bias was found, and so the "anchored" payment card was deemed to be a suitable device for the full-scale experiment.

Tests were also conducted to attempt to discover if any of the other sorts of bias were inherent in the questionnaire. Again, none was found.

A final point should be made regarding the payment card. What people actually pay for publicly provided goods varies with their income. To correct for this, four different payment cards were developed corresponding to four income classes. At the appropriate point in the interview, the interviewer gave the respondent the payment card for his or her income category, which had been established by a prior question.

As already discussed, the respondents valued three levels of water quality which were described in words and depicted on the water quality ladder. They were first asked how much they were willing to pay to maintain national water quality in the boatable level. Subsequent questions asked them their willingness to pay for overall water quality to fishable quality and swimmable quality. The average willingness-to-pay amounts given by the respondent for the two higher levels consists of the amounts they offered for the lower levels plus any additional amount they offered for the higher level.

The average annual amounts per household (1981 dollars) for those respondents who answered the willingness-to-pay questions turned out to be:

Water quality	Total $	Marginal $
Boatable	152	152
Fishable	194	42
Swimmable	225	31

The most substantial benefit is for boatable water. The respondents are willing to give about 20 percent more for fishable water than boatable water, but only an additional 15 percent to make the water swimmable. As we will see later, these are large amounts.

The data also permitted one to make a rough distinction between the type of recreation and the intrinsic values discussed earlier. Since the willingness-to-pay questions measure the overall value that respondents have for water quality, the amount given by each respondent represents the combination of recreational and intrinsic values held by that person. But it was possible to tell from the questions whether a person actually engaged in water-based recreation. It was reasoned that the values expressed by the respondents who do *not* engage in in-stream recreation should be almost purely intrinsic in nature. In calculating the average willingness-to-pay amount for the nonrecreationists alone, therefore, we get an approximation of the intrinsic value of water quality. By subtracting this amount from the total the recreationists are willing to pay, one can estimate, in a rough way, the portions of the recreationists' benefits which are attributable to recreation and intrinsic values.

When this is done, it is found that intrinsic value constitutes about 45 percent of the total value for recreationists, 100 percent for the nonrecreationists (by assumption), and about 55 percent for the sample as a whole. If this is a correct reflection of reality, it is a major finding and may have large implications for the future study of benefits from environmental improvement. This matter will be pursued further in chapter 11, in the section on visibility in the national parks.

It was noted earlier that, while the sample of persons interviewed was initially chosen at random, quite a few respondents failed to give usable answers. Any aggregate national benefit estimate based on these data therefore could not be put forward as accurate. Thus, I make such an estimate simply to illustrate that the results of this experiment imply very large values.

There are about 80 million households in the United States. Assume that the sample results imply that to have high-quality recreational waters throughout the country there is an annual willingness to pay of $200 per household. This would imply a total willingness to pay of $16 billion. According to the earlier discussion, this would divide about equally between user and nonuser values. At first this might seem out of line with the value of well under the billion dollars that was calculated for recreational fishing. But this is not necessarily the case. Recall that that estimate is for a relatively small *increase* in the nation's fishable waters over the actual conditions of the early 1970s, and that the estimate from the national survey is the value people attach to making and *maintaining* the whole of the nation's fresh waters of high recreational quality where the alternative is almost total degradation of most of the nation's watercourses. In other words, both the baselines and the routes of benefit accrual considered are different in the two studies. A somewhat closer comparison, though still not a perfect one, is between the survey's reported willingness to pay for an improvement from boatable to fishable water ($42 per household, or $3.4 billion) and the largest value found in the fishing study for essentially complete cleanup (in fishing terms) of the nation's *fresh* water—roughly $1 billion.

The objective of this experiment was not to produce an accurate estimate of national benefits, rather it was to test the feasibility of using a macro approach to the estimation of water-quality benefits. In that, it succeeded.

11

EMERGING AREAS FOR BENEFIT ESTIMATION
Visibility, Acid Rain, and Groundwater Contamination

Visibility in the National Parks

Visibility in the national parks primarily involves a preservation issue instead of one of amelioration. Historically, Americans have placed a high value on good visibility, that is, the ability to see distant objects clearly. This appreciation of atmospheric visual clarity is evidenced in the country's early literature and art, including the journals of Lewis and Clark as well as the masterpieces of the great American landscape artists of the nineteenth century. Today that yearning is demonstrated not only by the millions who flock each year to our western parks, but also in the high prices brought by those artists' works of a century ago and by the interest in Ansel Adams's simple, yet dramatically clear, black-and-white photographs of Yosemite and other wonders of the U.S. National Park System.

Over the past one hundred years, Congress has acted to preserve many of the nation's natural wonders. It did so by creating and by continually

AUTHOR'S NOTE: This section is based primarily on William D. Schulze, David S. Brookshire, Eric G. Walther, and Karen Kelley, *The Benefits of Preserving Visibility in the National Parklands of the Southwest,* Draft Report, vol. 8 of *Methods Development for Environmental Control Benefits Assessment* (Washington, D.C., U.S. Environmental Protection Agency, Office of Exploratory Research, Office of Research and Development, n.d.).

expanding the national parks, wilderness areas, monuments, recreation areas, and wild and scenic rivers.

Since the 1950s, there has been an increasing concern that this beauty is threatened by industrial development and population growth. Pollution from coal-fired power plants became a special concern in 1963 with the advent of the first unit of the Four Corners Power Plant near Farmington, New Mexico. It produced a plume that could be seen clearly for many miles, reducing the clarity of the visual experience in areas of northwestern New Mexico, southeastern Utah, southwestern Colorado, and northeastern Arizona.

By the later 1960s and the early 1970s, smog began to appear in Yosemite Valley, California, on warm summer days. Battles erupted over the visibility effects of proposed coal-fired power plants on the Kaiparowits Plateau and near Capitol Reef National Park, both in southern Utah. The increased publicity and concern resulted in magazine and newspaper articles decrying the loss of visual clarity, particularly in the western United States, and precipitated political pressures in Congress for legislative steps to protect visibility. Those pressures culminated in the August 1977 adoption by Congress of the nation's first specific visibility-protection requirements for national parks and national wilderness areas. One of the large issues raised by these developments is whether the value of visibility protection outweighs the cost, including both air pollution-control equipment and the regulatory system. The study reported in this section was designed to improve our ability to measure the benefits of visibility and to provide some preliminary estimates of the value of that visibility in several major national parks and for the region in which they are located. The Grand Canyon region and the parks located in it are shown in figure 11-1.

Visibility is the ability to see both color and detail over long distances. Human perception of visual air quality is associated with the apparent color contrast of distant visual targets. As contrast is reduced, a scene "washes out" both in terms of color and in one's ability to see distant detail. What, then, is the nature of the preservation value of visibility? That value has at least two possible components.

First, a scenic resource such as the Grand Canyon attracts large numbers of recreationists. The quality of the experience of these individuals depends in great part on air quality, in that scenic vistas are an integral part of the Grand Canyon "experience." Accordingly, the air quality at the Grand Canyon is valuable to recreationists. We might call this economic value, or willingness to pay by users for air quality at the Grand Canyon, *user value.* Thus, recreationists in the national parklands of the Southwest should be willing to pay some amount to preserve air quality for each day of their own use if their recreational experience is improved or maintained by good air quality.

The second component of preservation value we have termed *existence value.* (This concept was introduced in the abstract, in chapter 4, and has been explained in a more specific context in chapter 10.) Individuals and households who may never visit the Grand Canyon may still value visibility there simply because they wish to preserve a national treasure. Visitors also may wish to know that the Grand Canyon retains relatively pristine air quality even on days when they are not visiting the park. Concern over preserving the Grand Canyon may be just as intense in New York or Chicago as it is in nearby states and communities. Thus,

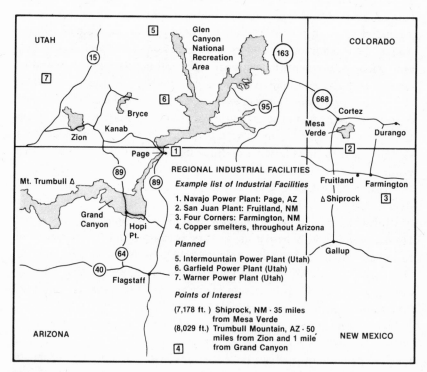

Figure 11-1. Relative location of national parks to industrial facilities in the Southwest.

preservation value has two additive components, user value and existence value.

During the summer of 1980, more than 600 people in Denver, Los Angeles, Albuquerque, and Chicago were shown five sets of photographs depicting both clear conditions and regional haze. Each set consisted of five photographs of a national park vista with different visual air quality of a general nature, that is, generally increased haziness. The vistas shown were from Grand Canyon, Mesa Verde, and Zion. Summer was chosen for the survey because it is the season of peak visitation.

These photographs were placed on display boards as full-frame, 8-×-10-inch textured prints, arranged from left to right in ascending order of visual air quality, with each vista in a separate row. Using the Grand Canyon vistas as an example, the manner in which these photographs were placed on the display boards is shown in figure 11-2.

The participants were asked how much they would be willing to pay for visibility as shown in the five sets of photographs, from worst to best. They were also asked how much they would be willing to pay to prevent a plume from being seen in a pristine area. Two photographs were used in this connection, one with and the other without a plume. The photographs were taken from Grand Canyon National Park at the Hopi fire tower observation point and toward Trumbull Mountain. They were both taken at 9:00 AM, so the lighting on the canyon wall and other features is the same. Both photographs have the same light, high cirrus cloud layer in the sky. The plume is a narrow gray band crossing the entire vista in the sky, except where it appears in front of the top of Trumbull Mountain. The source was not industrial or municipal pollution,

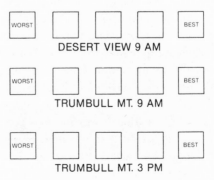

Figure 11-2. Grand Canyon photograph board.

but a controlled burn in the area around the Grand Canyon. However, the effect was comparable to what a large industrial source might produce.

The bidding game based on these photographs reveals the household's willingness to pay for preserving or improving the degree of visibility in specific locations of the national park area described earlier. The bids offered by respondents in the aggregate preservation-value section of the survey encompass both pure existence value and users' valuations of preserving visibility. Since the results did not permit a completely clean distinction between the two types of bids, further discussion will concentrate on the preservation-value section of the survey.

The benefits derived from the interview results can be extrapolated to populations larger than that in the sample (the sample was chosen in as random a manner as practical) by applying statistical techniques to the results of the survey. The amount of bids offered by interviewees to preserve or improve visibility is related to such factors as income, education, and other personal characteristics. These relationships can be quantified using regression analysis. After this is done, it is possible to estimate the value of benefits to residents of the whole Southwest region as well as the entire nation. This is done by substituting the average values for these characteristics for each state into the relationship established by the regression analysis and calculating what the average value of the bid of a person in that state would be. This value can then be multiplied by the population of the state as a whole to get a total bid.

When the analysis is performed for the southwestern United States (for residents of California, Colorado, Arizona, Utah, Nevada, and New Mexico), the following values are obtained. The figures show the annual willingness to pay for preserving present average conditions (figure 11-2, middle picture), as contrasted with the next worse condition depicted by the pictures, and for preventing plume blight. The aggregate benefits for the southwestern region from preserving visibility in the Grand Canyon National Park, the Grand Canyon region, and for avoiding a visible plume over the Grand Canyon are about $470, $889, and $373 million, respectively.

To estimate the aggregate national benefits from preserving visibility, a similar analysis is done for the entire United States, but additional survey data from Chicago are included, and the following values are obtained.

Annual benefits for	Total (million $)
Grand Canyon	3,370
The Grand Canyon region	5,760
The plume	2,040

These figures, even though their accuracy is highly uncertain, imply that very large existence values characterize the areas in question. However, some recent and highly preliminary experiments with surveys imply that these figures may be much too high. (This matter will be taken up again in chapter 12.)

Several other observations on the outcomes of the analysis of the actual interview results are worth mentioning here. First, in the conventional view of the demand for environmental quality, there is a smooth tradeoff between higher successive levels of environmental quality and economic benefits, with successive units commanding less incremental willingness to pay. This is embodied in the demand curves discussed in chapter 2, as is shown in figure 11-3.

The survey respondents, however, placed a much higher value on a small initial diminution in visual clarity than on comparable subsequent decreases. This produces a very unusual demand curve, resembling what mathematicians call a step function, something like figure 11-4.

Second, and again somewhat contrary to expectations, neither past nor prospective visits to the Grand Canyon region were shown to be important

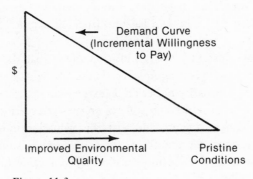

Figure 11-3.

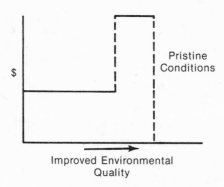

Figure 11-4.

determinants of preservation value. On the average, those who had never seen the Grand Canyon valued it as highly as those who had.

Third, and again unexpectedly, a household's distance from the region had no significant relationship to the size of its bids. When corrected for income and other differences, people in Chicago bid fully as high as those closer by. However, preliminary further investigation suggests that this result may not be very robust, being sensitive, for example, to the sequence in which people are asked about their valuation of various public goods. Further investigation is clearly indicated, and the matter will be discussed further in chapter 12.

Because the Grand Canyon is the dominant feature in a region with many visitor attractions, one must be especially cautious in extending these preliminary findings to other recreational attractions. It seems likely that there are only a very few natural phenomena in the United States about which Americans have such strong feelings. Obvious candidates for this short list would be Old Faithful (in Yellowstone National Park), Niagara Falls, and perhaps a few others.

The main conclusion of this visibility study is that the magnitude of the annual benefits, when aggregated across households, is impressive. While these are necessarily rather crude extrapolations, the survey results suggest that Americans place great value on the preservation of air quality in the Grand Canyon region, and that this valuation is not necessarily localized in the Southwest. Further, the survey results suggest that pure existence value may overwhelm a substantial user value for the national parks in the region.

Acid Rain

Acid rain and other mechanisms for the dispersion and deposition of acid formed from sulfur and nitrogen emitted from various sources are complex and ill-understood phenomena. In addition, methods for estimating the economic losses resulting from damages or economic benefits of prevention of acid rain are not well developed, nor was it possible within the scope of the project described here to make much progress in developing them.

Consequently, since the estimates of benefits made for controlling acid rain are very crude and of no particular interest in terms of methods development, the discussion here will be very brief. It is included primarily because of current intense interest in the phenomenon, and because the analysis that was done provides some guidance concerning directions for future research. Acid deposition, among all the areas covered in this volume, is perhaps the one most crying out for additional methods development and improved estimates. Let us turn first to its possible effects on agriculture and forestry.

Increases in soil acidity can negatively affect the yields of certain field crops, but this can be offset by modestly increasing liming operations which already occur for acid-sensitive crops. Therefore, the benefits of controlling acid rain for this purpose would be small. It is known that direct damage to the plant can occur from acid deposits on leaves, flowers, and fruits, but there is virtually no basis for estimating the amount of such an effect.

Forest growth can be affected in a similar fashion in that there can be both indirect effects, through the soil, as well as direct effects. As in the case of certain field crops, there may even be short-run favorable effects, for example, when the acid dissolves plant nutrients and makes them more available to the trees. Nonetheless, in the longer term this could result in reduced soil fertility and slower tree growth. If some strong assumptions are made, an estimate can be made of damages resulting from retarded growth. If one assumes—and there is some evidence

AUTHOR'S NOTE: This section is based primarily on Thomas D. Crocker, John T. Tschirhorst, Richard M. Adams, and Bruce Forster, *Methods Development for Assessing Acid Deposition Control Benefits*, vol. 7 of *Methods Development for Environmental Control Benefits Assessment* (Washington, D.C., U.S. Environmental Protection Agency, Office of Health and Ecological Effects, Office of Research and Development, n.d.).

pointing in this direction from Swedish studies—that acid rain would reduce timber growth in Minnesota and east of the Mississippi (the area of the country thought to be most affected by acid) by 5 percent annually, the reductions in yield would decrease the worth of timber production about $600 million per year. Assuming that other services of forests, such as watershed protection, fishing, and hunting, also were to be reduced by 5 percent, and based on crude estimates by others of the possible overall value of these services, the total damage including timber and other services might come to about $1.75 billion. This is a substantial sum, but not very large relative to the costs of controlling acid deposition.

There might also be effects on human health, say, by the acid dissolving and mobilizing heavy metals so that larger concentrations would get into drinking water or the human food chain. The present state of knowledge does not permit even very crude estimates to be made of this possibility. Higher acidity in municipal and industrial water systems might also result in increased corrosion in piping, appliances, and cooling systems. But the diminishing acidity in such systems, by the use of lime, is a routine operation and can be accomplished at small cost.

The big danger in watercourses appears to be those features of the aquatic ecosystem itself which mankind values. Acid conditions in a watercourse tend to destroy the small plants and animals (plankton), that are the initial links in the fish food chain, and this has a negative effect on fish population. But the primary way in which fish populations are destroyed is different. As noted earlier, acid in water bodies tends to mobilize toxic metals and increase their concentration in the water. The reproductive capacity of many species of animals, including fish, is adversely affected by the presence of excessive amounts of toxic metals. Thus, for a time, as fish numbers decline, the ones that remain increase in size as competition for food declines, but then rather abruptly there are none left. This, of course, destroys commercial and recreational fisheries. The value of fish taken by commercial freshwater fishing in the United States is not very large, so the loss there, at least as measured by present market prices, would not be very great.

On the other hand, the value of freshwater recreational fisheries is relatively enormous. Let us make the extreme assumption that all such fisheries in Minnesota and other areas east of the Mississippi would totally disappear. If we then take estimates of willingness to pay for fishing from other studies, it appears that the loss could, at an outside limit, be on the order of $10 billion per year in 1979 prices. Additional losses would be caused by the decline of terrestrial and aquatic animals (other than fish) who are partly or wholly dependent on the aquatic food chain—certain species of water fowl, for example.

The other area where our study suggests really major damages might occur is deleterious effects on materials. As noted previously, acid corrodes metals, eats away limestone, is harmful to paints and other coatings and finishes, and damages cloth. Given the huge number of such items which exist and are exposed to the atmosphere, it is not very surprising that benefits from protecting them might be large. Again, in Sweden, where the problems of acid rain first received widespread attention (because of prevailing winds, Sweden gets inputs of sulfur and nitrogen compounds from the Ruhr, the Rotterdam petrochemical complex, and Great Britain), a study has been made of per capita damages of corrosion and soiling. If one makes the assumption, once again very gross, that this same estimate can be applied to all persons dwelling in Minnesota and east of the Mississippi, one gets an annual benefit from avoiding acid rain of about $14 billion.

Putting together the various dollar estimates (agriculture, $1.75 billion; aquatic ecosystems, $10 billion; and materials damage, $14 billion), the benefits of preventing acid rain in 1978 dollars amounts to nearly $26 billion—a hefty amount indeed. But as stated, many extreme assumptions were made in generating these numbers, and they are no doubt too high by far. An educated guess by the research team was that the actual figure is probably not more than $5 billion for a condition that is characterized by severe effects on the entire eastern United States.

Of course this number cannot be taken very seriously, because even if it were correct, in all other respects it neglects the large adjustments in demand and supply which would accompany the types of changes contemplated. An approach much more like that described for the agriculture study in the South Coast Basin (see chapter 8) would be appropriate in a more sophisticated study.

Where are the greatest potential benefits of protection from acid rain likely to lie? These are, in rough order, materials damage, aquatic ecosystems effects, and effects on agriculture and forestry. These categories of damages certainly merit further study.

But our progress in economic research on these questions is highly dependent on improved dose-response relationships. As indicated in chapter 4, the relationship between the intrusion of acid into a watercourse and its ultimate effect appears to be extraordinarily complex. For example, what sudden changes could occur after a previously uneventful period, and what difficulties would be encountered in reversing them after they have occurred? Indeed, could they be reversed completely? Ecologists place great value on diversity of species as an indicator of a healthy, stable ecological system. Acidification of streams is known to reduce diversity. But it is not well understood how this ultimately affects characteristics of the stream that we value. This problem seems ripe for joint work between economists and ecologists.

Groundwater Contamination

While the extent of groundwater contamination is not accurately known, it is thought to be widespread and is the focus of much public apprehension. Contaminants in groundwater range across an enormous list of chemical substances, and usually no thorough checks for contamination are made until there is reason to suspect a problem.

Even at extremely low concentrations, many toxic chemicals pose serious, irreversible, health risks. In many of the cases investigated, well water has been found to contain concentrations above, and often several orders of magnitude higher than, those commonly encountered in raw or treated drinking water drawn from contaminated surface sources.

Thus, while water from most wells no doubt is safe, the widespread nature of the contamination and its potential seriousness merit the public attention the problem is getting. The intent of the case study in this chapter is to develop methods for estimating benefits from preventing contamination of groundwater-based drinking-water supplies. This, so far as I know, is the first study to attempt to quantify such benefits. As in the studies discussed in other chapters, the quantitative results reported here must be regarded as largely experimental, but the numbers turn out to be impressively large.

For any chemical source, the extent of groundwater contamination is determined by the characteristics of the underground storage medium—called an aquifer. Groundwater in shallow, alluvial aquifers typically moves less than a foot per day. That flow is governed by recharge and discharge rates from the aquifer, and by the aquifer's permeability.

AUTHOR'S NOTE: This section is based primarily on Mark F. Sharefkin, "Economic Benefits from Control of Major Environmental Episodes" (Washington, D.C., U.S. Environmental Protection Agency, Office of Research and Development, 1983).

Contaminants are transported by diffusion together with the slow underground flow of groundwater. In that oxygen-poor environment, chemical or physical processes of contaminant degradation proceed very slowly. Thus the contaminant plume may move great distances, with hardly a change in toxicity levels, and may therefore reach drinking-water wells.

Among the principal sources of groundwater contamination are waste-disposal landfills and impoundments, accidental spills of chemical substances, and abandoned oil and gas wells. Most groundwater contamination can be traced to chemicals leaching into the aquifer from poorly constructed and managed industrial or municipal landfills, surface impoundments, or outright illegal dumps. Contamination from such sources has often been in process for years, and sometimes for decades. To date, most groundwater contamination incidents have been discovered only after a drinking-water source has been affected. By the time suspected aquifer contamination is verified in samples drawn from drinking-water wells, the problem may be irreversible. Stricter regulation of the disposal of potential contaminants in other environmental media, particularly air and surface waters, and the consequent rising cost of such disposal, is likely to increase the flow of wastes to land disposal and aggravate the threat to groundwater.

Benefit analysis of controlling groundwater contamination requires, as usual, quantification of several link between sources and receptors. One must know the location and strength of actual or potential sources of contamination, and must be able to model the spread of the contaminant plume in the aquifer. One must know the numbers of persons exposed to contaminated groundwater and the extent and timing of their exposures. One must know the "dose-response relationship," the nature and extent of health effects on the population at risk. And finally, one needs a way of converting health effects into monetary, or dollar, values.

We are far from being able to quantify these link between sources and receptors with precision. In each case, there is a need for substantially improved methods and data. With these cautions in mind, let us proceed to the case study of Price's landfill near Atlantic City, New Jersey.

Actually, while it is referred to as a landfill, this is a rather euphemistic term—dump would be a better word—but I shall stick with the conventional usage. Price's landfill occupies approximately 22 acres extending across the boundary of Egg Harbor Township and the town of Pleasantville, New Jersey. Until 1967, it functioned as a sand and gravel quarry. During 1968, when the pit was excavated to within approximately 2 feet of the water table, people from the surrounding area began to dump trash into it with the permission of the owner, Charles Price. In 1969 Price began commercial operations that continued until the landfill was closed in 1976.

In 1970 Price applied to the New Jersey Department of Environmental Protection for a license to conduct a sanitary landfill operation. The application listed the materials that Price intended to accept at the landfill, and specifically excluded "Chemicals (Liquid or Solid)." He was issued a certificate authorizing operation of a solid waste disposal facility.

In July 1972 authorities inspected the landfill, citing Price for accepting chemical wastes and formally advising him of the violation. Nonetheless, Price continued accepting significant quantities of chemical wastes until November 1972. After that date, no chemical wastes were disposed of at the landfill, although it continued in operation. In 1976 Price terminated the landfill operation and covered the site with fill material. The site has not been used since then.

But during the period from May 1971 to November 1972, Price accepted approximately 9 million gallons of toxic and flammable chemical and liquid wastes, either in drums or directly into the ground. Among others, these included glycolic, nitric, and sulfuric acid, caustics and spent caustic wastes, cesspool waste, chemical resins and other waste chemicals, chloroform, and cleaning solvents.

Price's Landfill is situated over the Cohansey aquifer, the principal source of Atlantic City's water supply, and the separation between landfill and aquifer is a relatively permeable layer. Waste from the landfill is free to leach into the aquifer; the direction of flow in the aquifer is eastward, toward Atlantic City's wells. Chemicals in the leachate therefore can be carried into the private and public water-supply wells, and people can be exposed to these chemicals in drinking water. Test wells drilled near the landfill by the EPA show that groundwater in the aquifer is contaminated and that the plume of contamination indeed is moving toward Atlantic City's wells.

But estimation of actual or potential human exposures requires either considerable information on, or heroic assumptions about, the mechanism by which toxics are transported from the source of contamination to the water-supply wells. This is the second linkage mentioned earlier. Shortly it will be clear why discussion of this linkage logically precedes the first quantification of the source of the contamination.

Efforts to understand and model the source to receptor linkages, called groundwater solute transport, are relatively recent. While there has been considerable earlier work on salinity transport, study of the more difficult cases of chemically reactive toxic groundwater contaminants is less advanced. Improvements in our ability to model these phenomena must be a prime objective for future research.

For purposes of analyzing the Price's landfill situation, the researchers chose and estimated numerically a technique called the Wilson–Miller solute-transport model. This relatively simple model was chosen because of time and funding limitations for the research. The model chosen does appear to fit the Price's landfill situation relatively well and has been judged adequate for conducting this experiment. Future research should determine whether more complex models yield substantially different results.

But to apply any solute transport model, it is first necessary to have so-called source-term information, that is, the amounts of material entering groundwater and their distribution over time. Much of the activity at Price's landfill was illegal. It therefore seems unlikely, to say the least, that careful records of what went into the pit were kept. Indeed, for a large number of chemical substances there is no information at all about the amounts that have been dumped there. Where such records exist, or if leaching rates are known or can be calculated, deliveries of pollutants to the aquifer can be estimated directly. In the situation exemplified by Price's landfill, which is typical of much groundwater contamination, there is only one way to estimate the quantity. Since we have information on what is already present in test wells drilled by the EPA, the solute-transport model can be run "backwards," so to speak, and used to infer what amount there had to be to produce the existing groundwater concentrations. This is why, logically, the discussion of the transport model precedes discussion of the source term.

The reader should be cautioned that this estimate, while necessary, is based on many assumptions and involves great uncertainty. Just to give one example, the procedure assumes that releases occur at a constant rate. This may not be true for some pollutants, and "slugs" may be released which cause transients of pollution in much higher concentrations than would be predicted by the model.

But given the computed source term, the model can be run "forward" to compute concentrations at any well drawing on the aquifer—the production wells of Atlantic City, for example—and for any time after some contaminant enters the aquifer. Those concentrations, and the times at which they are projected to occur, were computed for the wells from which Atlantic City's Municipal Water Authority pumps its water. Assuming that no mitigating action is taken, this provides the link that specifies the exposure of the population to contamination from Price's landfill.

To take the next step, one must have dose-response information—that is, the actual health risk stemming from the contamination. To make this link, information published by the EPA was used. There is a section of the Clean Water Act that requires the EPA to estimate excess cancer risks for 129 chemicals called *priority pollutants*. Many of these priority pollutants are leaching from Price's landfill into the Cohansey aquifer. Using this information, the probability of excess mortality from cancer was estimated for the population of Atlantic City. While this procedure is the best available based on existing information, the reader should be aware that, for this purpose, the risk factors provided by the EPA are both incomplete and very uncertain. For example, there are many pollutants that have been identified in groundwater that are not on the EPA list, and extrapolations from animal toxicity tests to human risks are quite uncertain. Additionally, it is assumed that each chemical risk is independent of each other chemical risk so that risks can simply be added up across chemical categories. It is well known that a synergistic effect can occur, making the combined toxicity of two chemicals greater than the sum of the effects of each one taken independently.

Again, with all these cautions in mind, I turn to the next, and final, step, the monetary evaluation of damages. The value of risk chosen by the researchers is a range that reflects the underlying uncertainty and reasonably well spans the range of values discussed in chapter 4. The values ranged from $100,000 to $1 million per death. These were then multiplied by the mortality numbers calculated in the risk analysis to obtain the total benefit from averting the damage which would otherwise emanate from Price's landfill. The total benefit ranges from $180 million to $1.8 billion (discounted present value).

Those are large amounts, and one must be clear about what they mean. Say that, at a site similar to Price's landfill, there is a comparable release of contaminants into a similar aquifer, and that the release goes unnoticed for two decades. Then there will be human exposures through drinking water, and incremental mortality risks faced by the exposed population over their remaining lifetimes. Valuing this incremental mortality risk produced the figures cited above. At a site at which groundwater contamination has already occurred, those figures represent the damages that might be avoided by measures taken to prevent future exposures, either by restricting access to, or by cleansing, the aquifer. Needless to say, those figures are impressively large. But such limited information as there is indicates that the costs of cleansing aquifers are always large and the cost of obtaining an alternate water supply may be large. This analysis, shaky as the numbers necessarily are, suggests that where groundwater contamination is affecting drinking water supplies, prevention is probably the best cure.

IV

CONCLUSION

12

CONCLUDING NOTES

It seems fair to claim that the research reported in this book marks a substantial step forward in our ability to address the issue of benefits from environmental quality improvement or maintenance. Methods have been developed or expanded, new data have been collected, case studies have been provided, and some highly preliminary estimates of national benefits from environmental improvement or maintenance have been presented. Furthermore, some broad insights have resulted from the work. While so far I have done my best to fairly state, in nontechnical terms, the findings of my colleagues in this enterprise, the following generalizations and interpretations are strictly my own.

First, while our national air-quality standards are based upon alleged health effects, it appears from the work reported here that we know very little about the health consequences of air pollution. The team's work on both aggregate and microepidemiology is consistent with air pollution as a source of acute effects on an important scale. However, human evidence of chronic effects is tenuous at best. This is not to say there are none, but conclusive demonstration of such effects, or lack thereof, awaits improved data and methods.

Second, while our air-quality standards are mostly founded on presumed health impacts, it appears—based on the limited evidence our studies were able to develop—that other economic damages from pollution may be fully as great or even much greater. Poor air quality appears to have a costly effect on materials, but so far the extent of the damage has defied accurate quantification. So far as preservation values are concerned, it appears that protecting visibility yields large benefits, especially in the West. In the East, preventing deterioration of watercourses through acid deposition appears to involve large benefits so far as recreational values are concerned. But, alas, we are some distance away from a complete and accurate quantification of these values.

The interviewing done in connection with the studies on visibility in the national parks and national water-quality benefits suggests that there also may be a large category of benefits which we have termed *intrinsic.* That is, people may be willing to pay for clean areas—in some cases on a really substantial scale—even if they do not benefit directly from their use. This may result from a feeling of national pride in having a clean environment, especially in areas of outstanding natural beauty or unusual cultural importance. Establishing these values in an accurate and complete manner is still on the frontier of benefits research.

In the area of water quality a large-scale simulation study suggests that the *additional* benefits to recreational freshwater fishing from marginal improvements in water quality, which have resulted from implementation of national policy, are not impressively large. This is because so much of the nation's fresh water is already fishable. However, an experimental national survey suggests that the willingness of the public to pay for improvements and maintenance of the quality of the nation's water is large—on the order of many billions of dollars per year. Our research also suggests that a large portion, perhaps half, of these benefits are of the nonuser, intrinsic variety. This further suggests that, in addition to the value that people may attach to some particularly treasured sites, they may also find a large intrinsic value in achieving certain nationally declared goals like "swimmable" waters virtually everywhere in the country. A full-scale, national water-quality survey, designed by members of the research team, should shed much additional light on the matter of both user and intrinsic benefits.

In addition, methods have been developed to study the agricultural benefits of controlling air pollution. In contrast to earlier studies, these take into account various economic adaptations and adjustments, for example, crop or variety switching and the elasticity of demand for agricultural products. Early findings suggest that while damages in a highly polluted specialty crop area such as southern California may be significant, the main source of benefits could come from reducing pollution in areas where major field crops such as soybeans and wheat are grown. This is because the total value of production of these crops is so huge that even a relatively small increase in yields is associated with large benefits.

The groundwater study implies that large benefits can be obtained from protecting areas of concentrated population, such as Atlantic City, from the toxic pollution of drinking water supplies. In most cases the benefits should easily outweigh the costs of preventive measures.

Finally, I would like to make some observations on methodology. The methods pursued in our studies can be divided into two broad classes—those based, however indirectly, on observed human behavior, and those based on asking questions about hypothesized situations. The former are based on actual actions such as travel to recreation sites and what one is willing to pay for housing. The attraction of the behavior-based methods is that they reflect responses to real, not hypothetical, situations and therefore are based on real, not hypothetical, decisions. But these behavior-based methods have equally real limitations. For one thing, they are not applicable to all situations of interest in environmental benefits evaluation, for example, protecting a beautiful vista from visual impairment. Further, they are limited to user benefits, and some of our research has suggested that intrinsic benefits may be of extreme importance as well.

For these reasons, one must resort to methods based on asking questions contingent on certain hypothetical situations. These are the contingent valuation methods of bidding games and other surveys. Inevitably, doubts arise about the accuracy of such methods, given the hypothetical nature of the situations they examine.

On the one hand our research tends to support the view that careful questionnaire design can control previously identified sources of bias (starting-point, strategic, and other bias), and the South Coast and San Francisco experiments tend to support the view that bidding games can provide reasonable indicators of benefits from hypothetical improvements in air quality, at least in certain instances. One reason may be that persons residing in the regions studied, especially the Los Angeles area, have a very clear understanding of the situation in which they find themselves and have mentally processed much information about it and have based their decisions upon it.

Very recent and highly preliminary experiments with bidding games have suggested that where this is not the case, a source of bias may exist that could have substantial implications for some bidding-game results. The visibility in the parks study is perhaps the prime candidate among those I have discussed.

Recall that one interesting result of the study was that the reported willingness to pay of respondents did not appear to diminish with distances, for example, those surveyed in Chicago were fully as willing to pay to protect visibility at the Grand Canyon in the initial survey as were those who were questioned in Denver. In one set of later experiments, based on such a small sample that the results should not be regarded as anything but suggestive of hypotheses for future research, further bidding games were conducted in those two cities. Instead of being asked questions only about willingness to pay for visibility in the national parks, respondents in both cities first were asked about their willingness to pay for other, closer-to-home, environmental public goods. When this was done in Chicago, willingness to pay for visibility in the national parks dropped sharply below the result found in the previous survey. In Denver this was not the case, perhaps because the questions about visibility were less hypothetical for those in Denver and therefore their answers were better thought out than was true of the Chicago respondents. In another set of experiments, persons were asked about their willingness to pay for a national improvement in water quality. Another sample was then asked about the same improvement in water quality plus an improvement in air quality. The respondents' willingness to pay for both was about the same as the first group's willingness to pay for water-quality improvement alone.

These kinds of highly experimental results have led members of the research team to speculate that people may have "mental accounts," one of which may be for environmental improvement. If this is the case, when asked about a hypothetical, but rather dramatic, environmental improvement, they may allocate everything in their environmental account to it, neglecting alternative environmental improvements which, if confronted with them, also would be regarded as valuable. An important further development in contingent valuation techniques will be to devise methods to structure them so as to avoid the one-issue-at-a-time procedure that so far has characterized their applications.

While I believe that the research reported here represents a significant improvement in our understanding of the economic values of environmental quality, much remains to be learned. Total accuracy in benefits estimation is an impossible dream, but I believe that the work done so far demonstrates that steady progress is feasible.

V

BIBLIOGRAPHY AND INDEX

REPORTS TO THE U.S.
ENVIRONMENTAL PROTECTION
AGENCY

The publications listed below comprise the primary source materials used in the preparation of this book.

Adams, Richard M., and Thomas D. Crocker. n.d. *The Value of Air Pollution Damages to Agricultural Activities in Southern California*, vol. 6 of *Methods Development for Environmental Control Benefits Assessment* (Washington, D.C., U.S. Environmental Protection Agency, Office of Health and Ecological Effects, Office of Research and Development). EPA-230-07-83-011.

Adams, Richard M., Narongsdakdi Thanavibulchai, and Thomas D. Crocker. 1979. *A Preliminary Assessment of Air Pollution Damages for Selected Crops Within Southern California*, vol. 3 of *Methods Development for Assessing Air Pollution Control Benefits* (Washington, D.C., U.S. Environmental Protection Agency, Office of Health and Ecological Effects, Office of Research and Development). EPA-600/5-79-001c.

Ben-David, Shaul, Reza Pazand, Thomas D. Crocker, Ralph C. d'Arge, Shelby Gerking, and William Schulze. n.d. *Six Studies of Health Benefits from Air Pollution Control*, vol. 2 of *Methods Development for Environmental Control Benefits Assessment* (Washington, D.C., U.S. Environmental Protection Agency). EPA-230-07-83-007.

Brookshire, David S., Ralph C. d'Arge, William D. Schulze, and Mark A. Thayer. 1979. *Experiments in Valuing Non-Market Goods: A Case Study of Alternative Benefit Measures of Air Pollution Control in the South Coast Air Basin of Southern California,* vol. 2 of *Methods Development for Assessing Tradeoffs in Environmental Management* (Washington, D.C., U.S. Environmental Protection Agency, Office of Health and Ecological Effects, Office of Research and Development). EPA-600/5-79-001b.

Brookshire, David S., Thomas D. Crocker, Ralph C. d'Arge, Shaul Ben-David, Allen V. Kneese, and William D. Schulze. 1979. *Executive Summary,* vol. 5 of *Methods Development for Assessing Air Pollution Control Benefits* (Washington, D.C., U.S. Environmental Protection Agency, Office of Health and Ecological Effects, Office of Research and Development). EPA-600/5-79-001e.

Brookshire, David S., William D. Schulze, Ralph C. d'Arge, Thomas D. Crocker, Shelby Gerking, with Mark A. Thayer. n.d. *Six Studies on Nonmarket Valuation Techniques,* vol. 3 of *Methods Development for Environmental Control Benefits Assessment* (Washington, D.C., U.S. Environmental Protection Agency). EPA-203-07-83-008.

Crocker, Thomas D., William Schulze, Shaul Ben-David, and Allen V. Kneese. 1979. *Experiments with Economics of Air Pollution Epidemiology,* vol. 1 of *Methods Development for Assessing Air Pollution Control Benefits* (Washington, D.C., U.S. Environmental Protection Agency, Office of Health and Ecological Effects, Office of Research and Development). EPA-600/5-79-001a.

Crocker, Thomas D., John T. Tschirhorst, Richard M. Adams, and Bruce Forster. n.d. *Methods Development for Assessing Acid Deposition Control Benefits,* vol. 7 of *Methods Development for Environmental Control Benefits Assessment* (Washington, D.C., U.S. Environmental Protection Agency, Office of Health and Ecological Effects, Office of Research and Development). EPA-230-07-83-011.

Cropper, Maureen L., Wiliam R. Porter, Burton J. Hansen, Robert A. Jones, and John G. Riley. 1979. *Studies on Partial Equilibrium Approaches to Valuation of Environmental Amenities,* vol. 4 of *Methods Development for Assessing Air Pollution Control Benefits* (Washington, D.C., U.S. Environmental Protection Agency, Office of Health and Ecological Effects, Office of Research and Development). EPA-600/5-19-001d.

Cummings, Ronald G., H. S. Burness, and R. D. Norton. n.d. *Measuring Household Soiling Damage from Suspended Air Particulates: A Methodological Inquiry,* vol. 5 of *Methods Development for Environmental Control Benefits Assessment* (Washington, D.C., U.S. Environmental Protection Agency, Office of Health and Ecological Effects, Office of Research and Development). EPA-230-07-83-010.

Kneese, Allen V. n.d. *Measuring the Benefits of Clean Air,* vol. 1 of *Methods Development for Environmental Control Benefits Assessment* (Washington, D.C., U.S. Environmental Protection Agency). EPA-230-07-83-004.

Kopp, Raymond J., William J. Vaughan, and Michael Hazilla. 1983. "Agricultural Sector Benefits Analysis for Ozone: Methods Evaluation and Demonstration," Final Report (Research Triangle Park, N.C., U.S. Environmental Protection Agency, Office of Air Quality Planning and Standards).

Loehman, Edna, David Boldt, and Kathleen Chaikin. 1980. *Study Design and Property Value Study,* vol. 1 of *Measuring the Benefits of Air Quality Improvements in the San Francisco Bay Area,* Report prepared for the U.S. Environmental Protection Agency (Menlo Park, Calif., SRI International). EPA-230-07-83-009.

Mitchell, Robert Cameron, and Richard T. Carson. 1981. "An Experiment in Willingness to Pay for Intrinsic Water Pollution Control Benefits," Report to the U.S. Environmental Protection Agency (Washington, D.C., Resources for the Future).

Portney, Paul R., and John Mullahey. 1983. "Ambient Ozone and Human Health: An Epidemiological Analysis," vols. I and II, Draft Final Report (Research Triangle Park, N.C., U.S. Environmental Protection Agency, Office of Air Quality Planning and Standards). EPA-68-02-358.

Schulze, William D., David S. Brookshire, Eric G. Walther, and Karen Kelly. n.d. *The Benefits of Preserving Visibility in the National Parklands of the Southwest,* Draft Report, vol. 8 of *Methods Development for Environmental Control Benefits Assessment* (Washington, D.C., U.S. Environmental Protection Agency, Office of Exploratory Research, Office of Research and Development). EPA-230-07-83-013.

Sharefkin, Mark F. 1983. "Economic Benefits from Control of Major

Environmental Episodes" (Washington, D.C., U.S. Environmental Protection Agency, Office of Research and Development).

Vaughan, William J. and Clifford S. Russell. 1982. *Freshwater Recreational Fishing: The National Benefits of Water Pollution Control* (Washington, D.C., Resources for the Future).

SUPPLEMENTARY READINGS

Public Goods, Externalities, and Consumer's Surplus

Bishop, Richard C., and Thomas A. Herberlein. 1979. "Measuring Values of Extra-Market Goods: Are Indirect Measures Biased?" *American Journal of Agriculture Economics* vol. 61 (December) pp. 926–930.

Bohm, Peter. 1970. "Pollution, Purification, and the Theory of External Effects," *Swedish Journal of Economics* vol. 72, pp. 153–166.

Bohm, Peter. 1972. "Estimating Demand for Public Goods: An Experiment," *European Economic Review* vol. 3, no. 2, pp. 111–130.

Bohm, Peter. 1979. "Estimating Willingness to Pay: Why and How?" *Scandanavian Journal of Economics* vol. 81, no. 2.

Bowen, Howard R. 1943. "The Interpretation of Voting in the Allocation of Economic Resources," *Quarterly Journal of Economics* vol. 58, pp. 27–48.

Brookshire, David S., Ralph C. d'Arge, William D. Schulze, and Mark Thayer. 1981. "Experiments in Valuing Public Goods," in V. Kerry Smith, ed., *Advances in Applied Microeconomics* (Greenwich, Conn., JAI Press).

Cicchetti, Charles J., Anthony C. Fisher, and V. Kerry Smith. 1976. "An Econometric Valuation of a Generalized Consumer Surplus Measure: The Mineral King Controversy," *Econometrica* (November) pp. 1259–1276.

Gordon, Irene M., and Jack L. Knetsch. 1979. "Consumer's Surplus Measures and the Evaluation of Resources," *Land Economics* vol. 55, no. 1 (February) pp. 1–10.

Harden, Russell. 1982. *Collective Action* (Baltimore, Md., Johns Hopkins University Press for Resources for the Future).

Just, R. E., D. L. Hueth, and A. Schmitz. 1982. *Applied Welfare Economics and Public Policy* (Englewood Cliffs, N.J., Prentice-Hall).

Kneese, Allen V., and Charles L. Schultze. 1975. *Pollution, Prices, and Public Policy* (Washington, D.C., Brookings Institution).

Laffont, Jean-Jacques, ed. 1977. *Aggregation and Revelation of Preferences* (Amsterdam, North-Holland).

Lin, Steven, ed. 1976. *Theory and Measurement of Economic Externalities* (New York, Academic Press).

Mäler, Karl-Göran, and Ronald E. Wyzga. 1976. *Economic Measurement of Environmental Damage* (Paris, Organisation for Economic Co-operation and Development).

Mulligan, P. J. 1977. "Willingness-to-Pay for Decreased Risk from Nuclear Plant Accidents," Working Paper No. 3 (University Park, Pennsylvania State University Energy Extension Program).

Pendse, Delip, and J. B. Whykoff. 1974. "Scope for Valuation of Environmental Goods," *Land Economics* vol. 50, no. 1 (February) pp. 89–92.

Scherr, Bruce A., and Emerson M. Babb. 1975. "Pricing Public Goods: An Experiment with Two Proposed Pricing Systems," *Public Choice* vol. 23 (Fall) pp. 35–48.

Schulze, W. D., R. C. d'Arge, and D. S. Brookshire. 1981. "Valuing Environmental Commodities: Some Recent Experiments," *Land Economics* vol. 58 (May) pp. 151–172.

Sinden, J. A., and A. C. Worrell. 1979. *Unpriced Values: Decisions Without Market Prices* (New York, John Wiley).

Willig, R. D. 1976. "Consumer's Surplus Without Apology," *The American Economic Review* vol. 6, no. 4 (September) pp. 589–597.

Acid Deposition

"Acid Rain Research—A Special Report." 1983. *EPRI Journal* (November).

Andersson, F. 1980. "Swedish Research on the Effects of Acid Deposition on Forests and Water." Paper presented at the International Conference on the Ecological Impact of Acid Precipitation, Oslo, Norway, March 11–14.

Appalachian Regional Commission. 1969. *Acid Mine Drainage in Appalachia* (Washington, D.C.).

Bengtsson, B. 1980. "Liming Acid Lakes in Sweden," *Ambio* vol. 9, pp. 34–36. Blake, L. M. n.d. *Liming Acid Ponds in New York* (Watertown, New York State Department of Environmental Conservation).

Carter, Luther J. 1979. "Uncontrolled SO_2 Emissions Bring Acid Rain," *Science* vol. 204 (June 15) pp. 1181–1182.

Cogbill, C. V. 1976. "The History and Character of Acid Precipitation in North America," *Water, Soil, and Air Pollution* vol. 6, pp. 407–413.

Comptroller General of the United States. 1981. *The Debate Over Acid Precipitation: Opposing Views, Status of Research* (Washington, D.C., Government Printing Office).

Dochinger, L. S., and T. A. Seliga, eds. 1976. *Proceedings of the First International Symposium on Acid Precipitation and the Forest Ecosystem* (Columbus, Ohio State University Press).

Galloway, J. N., and Others. 1978. *A National Program for Assessing the Problem of Atmospheric Deposition (Acid Rain)*, Report to the President's Council on Environmental Quality (Fort Collins, Colorado State University, National Atmospheric Deposition Program).

Gold, Peter S., ed. 1982. *Acid Rain: A Transjurisdictional Problem in Search of Solution* (Buffalo, Canadian-American Center, State University of New York).

Hendry, G., ed. 1978. *Limnological Aspects of Acid Precipitation*, BNL51074 (Upton, N.J., Brookhaven National Laboratory).

Jacobson, J. S. 1981. "Acid Rain and Environmental Policy," *Journal of the Air Pollution Control Association* vol. 31, pp. 1071–1093.

Johnson, D. W. 1981. *Acid Rain and Forest Productivity,* Pub. No. 1717 (Oak Ridge, Tenn., Oak Ridge National Laboratory).

Jonsson, B., and R. Sundberg. 1972. "Has the Acidification by Atmospheric Pollution Caused a Growth Reduction in Swedish Forests?" Res. Note No. 20 (Stockholm, Sweden, Department of Forest Yield Research, Royal College of Forestry).

Northeast Regional Task Force on Atmospheric Deposition. 1981. *Northeast Damage Report on the Long-Range Transport of Air Pollutants* (Boston, Mass.).

Patrick, R. V., P. Binetti, and S. G. Halterman. 1981. "Acid Lakes from Natural and Anthropogenic Causes," *Science* vol. 211 (January 30) pp. 446–448.

Wood, M. J. 1979. *Ecological Effects of Acid Precipitation,* Report of a workshop held at Gatehouse-of-Fleet, United Kingdom, September 4–7, 1978 (Surrey, U.K., Central Electricity Research Laboratories).

Air Pollution

Anderson, Robert C., and Bart Ostro. 1983. "Benefits Analysis and Air Quality Standards," *Natural Resources Journal* vol. 23, no. 3 (July) pp. 565–576.

Anderson, Robert J., Jr., and Thomas D. Crocker. 1971. "The Economics of Air Pollution: A Literature Assessment," in P. B. Downing, ed., *Air Pollution and the Social Sciences* (New York, Praeger) pp. 133–136.

Atkinson, S. E., and D. H. Lewis. 1974. "A Cost-Effectiveness Analysis of Alternative Air Quality Control Strategies," *Journal of Environmental Economics and Management* vol. 1, pp. 237–250.

Atkinson, S. E., and D. H. Lewis. 1976. "Determination and Implementation of Optimal Air Quality Standards," *Journal of Environmental Economics and Management* vol. 3 (September) pp. 363–380.

Barnes, R. A. 1979. "The Long-Range Transport of Air Pollution: A Review of the European Experience," *Journal of the Air Pollution Control Association* vol. 29 (December) pp. 1219–1235.

Barnett, L. B., and T. E. Waddell. 1973. *The Cost of Air Pollution Damages,* Pub. No. AP-85 (Research Triangle Park, N.C., U.S. Environmental Protection Agency).

Freeman, A. Myrick III. 1978. "Air and Water Pollution Policy," in Paul R. Portney, ed., *Current Issues in U.S. Environmental Policy* (Baltimore, Md., Johns Hopkins University Press for Resources for the Future).

Heintz, H. T., Jr., A. Hershaft, and G. C. Horok. 1976. *National Damages of Air and Water Pollution*, Report prepared for the U.S. Environmental Protection Agency (Rockville, Md., Enviro Control, Inc.).

McDougall, Gerald S., and Colin Wright. 1980. "A Proposal for Improving the Benefits from Pollution Abatement," *Journal of Environmental Economics and Management* vol. 7, no. 1 (March) pp. 20–29.

Mills, E. S., and L. White. 1978. "Auto Emissions: Why Regulation Hasn't Worked," *Technology Review* (April–May).

National Academy of Sciences. 1974. *Report by Committee on Motor Vehicle Emissions* (Washington, D.C., NAS).

National Academy of Sciences, Commission on Natural Resources. 1975. *Air Quality and Stationary Source Emission Control*, U.S. Senate Committee on Public Works, 94 Cong., 1st sess., Ser. 94-4 (Washington, D.C., Government Printing Office).

National Academy of Sciences and National Academy of Engineering. 1974. *Quality and Automobile Emissions Control*, vol. 4, *The Costs and Benefits of Automobile Emissions Control* (Washington, D.C., NAS).

National Commission on Air Quality. 1981. *To Breathe Clean Air, Report of the National Commission on Air Quality* (Washington, D.C., Government Printing Office).

Ridker, Ronald G. 1967. *Economic Costs of Air Pollution* (New York, Praeger).

Rowe, Robert D., and Lorraine G. Chestnut, eds. 1983. *Managing Air Quality and Scenic Resources at National Parks and Wilderness Areas* (Boulder, Colo., Westview Press).

Ryan, John W. 1981. *An Estimate of Nonhealth Benefits of Meeting the Secondary National Ambient Air Quality Standards* (Palo Alto, Calif., Stanford Research Institute, Inc.).

Seinfeld, John H. 1975. *Air Pollution: Physical and Chemical Fundamentals* (New York, McGraw-Hill).

Smith, V. Kerry. 1977. *The Economic Consequences of Air Pollution* (Cambridge, Mass., Ballinger).

Stern, A. C., ed. 1977. *Air Pollution* (3 ed., New York, Academic Press).

Waddell, T. E. 1974. *The Economic Damages of Air Pollution, Socioeconomic Environmental Studies Series* (Washington, D.C., U.S. Environmental Protection Agency).

White, Lawrence J. 1982. *The Regulation of Air Pollutants Emissions from Motor Vehicles* (Washington, D.C., American Enterprise Institute for Public Policy Research).

Benefit–Cost Analysis

Babcock, Lyndon R., and Miren L. Nagda. 1973. "Cost-Effectiveness of Emission Control," *Journal of the Air Pollution Control Association* vol. 23, no. 3 (March) pp. 173–179.

Barnes, David W. 1983. "Back-door Cost–Benefit Analysis Under a Safety-First Clean Air Act, *Natural Resources Journal* vol. 23, no. 4 (October) pp. 827–858.

Baumol, W. J., and W. E. Oates. 1979. *Economics, Environmental Policy, and the Quality of Life* (Englewood Cliffs, N.J., Prentice-Hall).

Bradford, David F. 1970. "Benefit–Cost Analysis and the Demand for Public Goods," *Kyklos* vol. 23, p. 775.

Brookshire, David S., and Thomas D. Crocker. 1981. "The Advantages of Contingent Valuation Methods for Benefit–Cost Analysis," *Public Choice* vol. 36, pp. 235–252.

Buchanan, J. 1969. *Cost and Choice* (Chicago, Ill., Markham).

Burness, H. Stuart, Ronald G. Cummings, A. F. Mehr, and M. S. Walbert. 1983. "Valuing Policies Which Reduce Environmental Risk," *Natural Resources Journal* vol. 23, no. 3 (July) pp. 675–682.

Carson, Richard T., and Robert Cameron Mitchell. 1983. "Observations on Strategic Bias and Contingent Valuation Surveys" (Washington, D.C., Resources for the Future).

Costs and Benefits of Environmental Protection. 1981. (Canberra, Australian Government Publishing Service).

Courant, Paul N., and Richard Porter. 1981. "Averting Expenditure and the Cost of Pollution," *Journal of Environmental Economics and Management* vol. 8, pp. 321–329.

Freeman, A. Myrick III. 1982. *Air and Water Pollution Control: A Benefit–Cost Assessment* (New York, John Wiley).

Freeman, A. Myrick, III. 1979. "The Benefits of Air and Water Pollution Control: A Review and Synthesis of Recent Estimates," Report prepared for the Council on Environmental Quality (Washington, D.C., CEQ).

Freeman, A. Myrick III. 1979. *The Benefits of Environmental Improvement* (Baltimore, Md., Johns Hopkins University Press for Resources for the Future).

Gramlich, Edward M. 1981. *Benefit–Cost Analysis of Government Programs* (Englewood Cliffs, N.J., Prentice-Hall).

Halvorsen, R., and M. G. Ruby. 1983. *Benefit–Cost Analysis of Air Pollution Control* (Lexington, Mass., Lexington Books).

Mathtech, Inc. 1982. *Benefits Analysis of Alternative Secondary National Ambient Air Quality Standards for Sulfur Dioxide and Total Suspended Particulates* (Princeton, N.J., Mathtech, Inc.).

Mills, E. S., ed. 1975. *Economic Analysis and Environmental Problems* (New York, Columbia University Press for NBER).

National Academy of Sciences, Coordinating Committee on Air Quality Studies. 1974. *The Costs and Benefits of Automobile Emission Control,* vol. 4 of *Air Quality and Automobile Emission Control,* Series No. 19-27 (Washington, D.C., NAS).

Peskin, Henry M., and Eugene P. Seskin, eds. 1975. *Cost–Benefit Analysis of Water Pollution Policy* (Washington, D.C., Urban Institute).

Randall, Alan, John P. Hoehn, and David S. Brookshire. 1983. "Contingent Valuation Surveys for Evaluating Environmental Assets," *Natural Resources Journal* vol. 23, no. 3 (July).

Ruff, L. E. 1970. "The Economic Common Sense of Pollution," *The Public Interest* vol. 19, pp. 69–85.

Runge, Carlisle Ford. 1983. "Risk Assessment and Environmental Benefits Analysis," *Natural Resources Journal* vol. 23, no. 3 (July) pp. 683–696.

Schwing, R. C., W. S. Bradford, C. R. Von Busek, and C. J. Jackson. 1980. "Benefit–Cost Analysis of Automotive Emission Reductions," *Journal of Environmental Economics and Management* vol. 7, no. 1 (March).

Swartzman, Daniel, Richard Leroff, and Kevin Croke, eds. 1982. *Cost–Benefit Analysis and Environmental Regulations* (Washington, D.C., Conservation Foundation).

Effect of Pollution on Agriculture

Water Resources Council. 1983. *Economic and Environmental Principles and Guidelines for Water and Related Land Resources Implementation Studies* (Washington, D.C., Government Printing Office).

Adams, Richard M., and Thomas D. Crocker. 1982. "Dose-Response Information and Environmental Damage Assessments: An Economic Perspective," *Journal of the Air Pollution Control Association* vol. 32, pp. 1062–1067.

Adams, Richard M., Thomas D. Crocker, and Narongsdakdi Thanvibulchai. 1982. "An Economic Assessment of Air Pollution Damages to Selected Annual Crops in Southern California," *Journal of Environmental Economics and Management* vol. 9 (February) pp. 45–58.

Benedict, H. M., C. J. Miller, and J. S. Smith. 1973. *Assessment of Economic Impact of Air Pollutants on Vegetation in the United States—1969 and 1971* (Menlo Park, Calif., Stanford Research Institute).

Carriere, W. M., A. D. Hinkley, W. Harshbarger, J. Kinsman, and J. Wisniewski. 1982. "The Effect of SO_2 and O_3 on Selected Agricultural Crops," Report prepared for the Electric Power Research Institute (McLean, Va., General Research Corporation).

Crocker, Thomas D., B. L. Dixon, R. E. Howitt, and R. Oliveria. 1981. "A Program for Assessing the Economic Benefits of Preventing Air Pollution Damages to U.S. Agriculture," Discussion Paper prepared for the National Crop Loss Assessment Network (NCLAN), (Laramie, University of Wyoming).

Heck, W. W., O. C. Taylor, R. Adams, G. Bingham, J. Miller, E. Preston, and L. Weinstein. 1982. "Assessment of Crop Loss from Ozone," *Journal of the Air Pollution Control Association* vol. 32, no. 4, pp. 353–361.

Heck, W. W., O. C. Taylor, R. Adams, G. Bingham, J. E. Miller, and L. H. Weinstein. 1981. *National Crop Loss Assessment Network 1980 Annual Report* (Corvallis, Ore., U.S. Environmental Protection Agency, Environmental Research Laboratory, Office of Research and Development).

Jacobsen, J. S. and A. A. Miller, eds. 1982. *Effects of Air Pollution on Farm Commodities* (Arlington, Va., Izaak Walton League of America) pp. 103–124.

Johnston, W. E., and G. W. Dean. 1969. *California Crop Trends: Yields, Acreages, and Production Areas,* California Agricultural Experiment Station, Extension Service Circular 555 (Berkeley, University of California).

Research Management Committee. 1982. *The National Crop Loss Assessment Network (NCLAN): 1981 Annual Report* (Corvallis, Ore., Environmental Research Laboratory, U.S. Environmental Protection Agency).

Southern California Association of Governments and South Coast Air Quality Management District. 1979. *Air Quality Management Plan.*

Thomas, M. D. 1961. "Effects of Air Pollution on Plants," in *Air Pollution,* World Health Organization Monograph Series No. 46 (New York, Columbia University Press) pp. 233–278.

Effect of Pollution on Ecosystems

Arrow, Kenneth J., and Anthony C. Fisher. 1974. "Environmental Preservation, Uncertainty, and Irreversibility," *Quarterly Journal of Economics* vol. 88 (May) pp. 302–319.

Crocker, Thomas D., John T. Tschirhorst, and Richard M. Adams. 1980. "Valuing Ecosystem Functions: The Effects of Acidification." Paper prepared for Redistributive Impact in the Federal Acid Rain Program, Denver, Colo., September 5.

Fisher, Anthony C., and John V. Krutilla. 1974. "Valuing Long-Run Ecological Consequences and Irreversibilities," *Journal of Environmental Economics and Management* vol. 1 (June) pp. 96–108.

Fisher, Anthony C., John V. Krutilla, and Charles J. Cicchetti. 1972. "The Economics of Environmental Preservation: A Theoretical and Empirical Analysis," *American Economic Review* vol. 62, pp. 605–619.

Hagerhill, B. 1979. "Estimation of Economic Damages to Aquatic Ecosystems in Sweden in Relation to Different Emissions Control Cases for 1985." Paper prepared for the Organisation of European Co-operation and Development Workshop on Acid Precipitation, Paris, France, April 24–26.

Hirschlefer, Jack. 1977. "Economics from a Biological Standpoint," *The Journal of Law and Economics* vol. 20 (April) pp. 1–52.

Hutchinson, T. C., and M. Havas, eds. 1980. *Effects of Acid Precipitation on Terrestrial Ecosystems* (New York, Plenum Press).

Kneese, Allen V. 1976. "Analysis of Environmental Pollution," *Swedish Journal of Economics* vol. 3, pp. 253–288.

Kormondy, E. J. 1969. *Concepts of Ecology* (Englewood Cliffs, N.J., Prentice-Hall).

Tullock, Gordon. 1971. "Biological Externalities," *Journal of Theoretical Biology* vol. 33, pp. 565–576.

Woodwell, G. M. 1970. "Effects of Pollution on the Structure and Physiology of Ecosystems," *Science* vol. 168 (April) p. 429–433.

Effect of Pollution on Human Health

Arthur, W. B. 1981. "The Economics of Risks to Life," *American Economic Review* vol. 71, no. 1 (March).

Bailey, Martin J. 1980. *Reducing Risks to Life: Measurement of the Benefits* (Washington, D.C., American Enterprise Institute).

Bhagia, Gobend S., and Herbert Stoevener. 1978. *Impact of Air Pollution on Consumption of Medical Services* (Corvallis, Ore., U.S. Environmental Protection Agency).

Bouhuys, A., G. J. Beck, and J. B. Schoenberg. 1978. "Do Present Levels of Air Pollution Outdoors Affect Respiratory Health?" *Nature* vol. 276 (November 30) pp. 466–471.

Carpenter, Ben H., D. A. LeSourd, James R. Chromy, and Walter D. Boch. 1977. *Health Costs of Air Pollution Damages, A Study of Hospitalization Costs* (Research Triangle Park, N.C., U.S. Environmental Protection Agency).

Christiansen, G., and C. Degan. 1980. "Air Pollution and Mortality Rates: A Note on Lave and Seskin's Pooling of Gross-Section and Time-Series Data," *Journal of Environmental Economics and Management* vol. 7, no. 2 (June) pp. 149–155.

Colmar, C. L., and L. A. Sagan. 1976. "Health Effects of Energy Production and Conversion," in J. M. Hollander, ed., *Annual Review of Energy* vol. 1, pp. 581–600.

Freeman, A. Myrick III. 1982. "The Health Implications of Residuals Discharges: A Methodological Overview," in V. Kerry Smith and John V. Krutilla, eds., *Explorations in Natural Resource Economics*

(Baltimore, Md., Johns Hopkins University Press for Resources for the Future).

Goldsmith, J. R., and L. T. Fribert. 1977. "Effects of Air Pollution on Human Health," in A. C. Stern, ed., *The Effects of Air Pollution* (3 ed., New York, Academic Press).

Gotchy, R. L. 1977. "Health Effects Attributable to Coal and Nuclear Fuel Cycle Alternatives" (Washington, D.C., U.S. Nuclear Regulatory Commission).

Higgins, I. T. T. 1974. *Epidemiology of Chronic Respiratory Disease: A Literature Review*, Environmental Health Effects Research Series, EPA-650/1-74-007 (Research Triangle Park, N.C., U.S. Environmental Protection Agency).

Kneese, Allen V., and William Schulze. 1977. "Environment, Health, and Economics—The Case of Cancer," *American Economic Review* no. 67 (February) pp. 26–32.

Lave, Lester B., and Eugene P. Seskin. 1970. "Air Pollution and Human Health," *Science* vol. 169 (August) pp. 723–733.

—. 1977. *Air Pollution and Human Health* (Baltimore, Md., Johns Hopkins University Press for Resources for the Future).

Lipfert, F. 1980. "Sulfur Oxides, Particulates and Human Mortality: Synopsis of Statistical Correlation," *Journal of the Air Pollution Control Association* vol. 31.

National Academy of Sciences. Committee on Medical and Biological Effects of Environmental Pollutants. 1977. *Ozone and Other Photochemical Oxidants* (Washington, D.C., NAS).

Ostro, Bart D. 1983. "The Effects of Air Pollution on Work Loss and Morbidity," *Journal of Environmental Economics and Management* vol. 10, no. 4 (December) pp. 371–382.

Page, Talbot, Robert Harris, and Samuel S. Epstein. 1976. "Drinking Water and Cancer Mortality in Louisiana," *Science* vol. 193, no. 4247 (July) pp. 55–57.

Perara, Frederick P., and A. Karim Ahmed. 1979. *Respirable Particles: Impact of Airborne Fine Particulates on Health and the Environment* (Cambridge, Mass., Ballinger) pp. 31–44.

Seskin, Eugene P. 1979. "An Analysis of Some Short-Term Health Effects of Air Pollution in the Washington, D.C., Metropolitan Areas," *Journal of Urban Economics* vol. 6 (July) p. 275–291.

Thibodeau, L. 1980. "Air Pollution and Human Health: A Review and Reanalysis," *Environmental Health Perspectives* vol. 34.

U.S. Environmental Protection Agency. 1974. *Health Consequences of Sulfur Oxides: A Report from CHESS, 1970–71* (Research Triangle Park, N.C., EPA Human Studies Laboratory).

Viren, John R. 1978. *Cross-Sectional Estimates of Mortality Due to Fossil Fuel Pollutants: A Case for Spurious Association* (Washington, D.C., U.S. Department of Energy).

Effect of Pollution on Materials

Booz-Allen and Hamilton, Incorporated. 1970. *Study to Determine Residential Soiling Costs of Particulate Air Pollution* (Washington, D.C.).

Crocker, Thomas D., and Ronald G. Cummings. 1983. "On Valuing Deposition-Induced Materials Damages: A Methodological Inquiry" (Laramie, University of Wyoming).

Gillette, Donald D. 1975. "Sulfur Dioxide and Material Damage," *Journal of the Air Pollution Control Association* vol. 25, no. 12 (December) pp. 1238–1243.

Watson, William D., and John A. Jaksch. 1982. "Air Pollution: Household Soiling and Consumer Welfare Losses," *Journal of Environmental Economics and Management* vol. 9, no. 3 (September) pp. 248–262.

Yocon, V. E., and N. Grappone. 1976. "The Effects of Power Plant Emissions on Materials," Report prepared by the Research Corporation of New England (Palo Alto, Calif., Electric Power Research Institute).

Effect of Pollution on Property Values

Abelson, Peter W. 1979. "Property Prices and the Value of Amenities," *Journal of Environmental Economics and Management* vol. 6, no. 1 (March) pp. 1–10.

Anderson, Robert J., and Thomas D. Crocker. 1971. "Air Pollution and Residential Property Values," *Urban Studies* No. 8 (October) pp. 171–180.

Brigham, Eugene F. 1965. "The Determinants of Residential Land Values," *Review of Economics and Statistics* vol. 59 (August) pp. 272–278.

Deyoh, Timothy, and V. Kerry Smith. 1974. "Residential Property Values and Air Pollution: Some New Evidence," *Quarterly Review of Economics and Business* vol. 14 (Winter) pp. 93–100.

Freeman, A. Myrick III. 1971. "Air Pollution and Property Values: A Methodological Comment," *Review of Economics and Statistics* vol. 53, pp. 415–416.

Freeman, A. Myrick III. 1974. "On Estimating Air Pollution Control Benefits from Land Value Studies, *Journal of Environmental Economics and Management* vol. 1, no. 1 (May) pp. 74–83.

Harris, R. N. S., G. S. Tolley, and C. Harrell. 1968. "The Residence Site Choice," *Review of Economics and Statistics* vol. 50 (May) pp. 241–247.

Harrison, David, Jr., and Daniel L. Rubinfeld. 1978. "The Air Pollution and Property Value Debate," *Review of Economics and Statistics* vol. 60, no. 4 (November) pp. 635–638.

Harrison, David, Jr., and Daniel L. Rubinfeld. 1978. "Hedonic Housing Prices and the Demand for Clean Air," *Journal of Environmental Economics and Management* vol. 5, no. 2 (March) pp. 81–102.

Hoch, Irving. 1977. "Variations in the Quality of Urban Life Among Cities and Regions," in Lowden Wingo and Alan Evans, eds., *Public Economics and the Quality of Life* (Baltimore, Md., Johns Hopkins University Press for Resources for the Future) pp. 28–65.

Nelson, J. 1979. "Airport Noise, Location Rent, and the Market for Residential Amenities," *Journal of Environmental Economics and Management* vol. 6 (December) pp. 320–331.

Niskanen, W. A., and S. H. Hanke. 1977. "Land Prices Substantially Underestimate the Value of Environmental Quality," *Review of Economics and Statistics* vol. 59, pp. 375–377.

Polinsky, A. M., and S. Shavell. 1975. "The Air Pollution and Property Value Debate," *Review of Economics and Statistics* vol. 57, pp. 100–104.

Portney, Paul R. 1981. "Housing Prices, Health Effects, Valuing Reductions in Risk to Death," *Journal of Environmental Economics and Management* vol. 8, pp. 72–78.

Ridker, Ronald G., and John Henning. 1967. "The Determinants of Residential Property Values With Special Reference to Air

Pollution," *Review of Economics and Statistics* vol. 49 (May) pp. 246–257.

Small, K. A. 1975. "Air Pollution and Property Values: A Further Comment," *Review of Economics and Statistics* vol. 57, pp. 105–107.

Smith, V. Kerry, and Timothy A. Deyak. 1975. "Measuring the Impact of Air Pollution on Property Values, *Journal of Regional Science* vol. 15, no. 3, pp. 277–288.

Tolley, George S., and Allen S. Cohen. 1976. "Air Pollution and Urban Land Use Policy, *Journal of Environmental Economics and Management* vol. 2, pp. 247–254.

Wieand, K. F. 1973. "Air Pollution and Property Values: A Study of the St. Louis Area," *Journal of Regional Science* vol. 13, pp. 91–95.

Effects of Pollution on Visibility

Blank, F., David S. Brookshire, Thomas D. Crocker, Ralph C. d'Arge, R. Horst, Jr., and R. Rowe. 1977. *Valuation of Aesthetic Preferences: A Case Study of the Economic Value of Visibility* (Laramie, University of Wyoming, Resource and Environmental Economics Laboratory).

Brookshire, David S., Berry C. Ives, and William D. Schulze. 1976. "The Valuation of Aesthetic Preferences," *Journal of Environmental Economics and Management* vol. 3, no. 4 (December).

Brookshire, David S., William D. Schulze, and E. G. Walther. 1983. "The Economic Benefits of Preserving Visibility in the National Parklands of the Southwest," *Natural Resources Journal* vol. 23 (January) pp. 149–173.

Charles River Associates, Incorporated. 1980. "Visibility Impairment at Mesa Verde National Park: An Analysis of Benefits and Costs of Controlling Emissions in the Four Corners Area," Report prepared for the Electric Power Research Institute (Palo Alto, Calif., EPRI).

Charlson, R. 1978. "Seven Authorities Speak Out on Visibility," Report prepared for the National Park Service, U.S. Department of the Interior (Washington, D.C., Government Printing Office).

Rae, Douglas A. 1982. "The Value to Visitors of Improving Visibility at Mesa Verde and the Great Smoky National Parks," in Robert D. Rowe and Lauraine G. Chestnut, eds., *Managing Air Quality and Visual Resources at National Parks and Wilderness Areas* (Boulder, Colo., Westview Press).

Randall, Alan, Berry Ives, and Clyde Eastman. 1974. *Benefits of Abating Aesthetic Environmental Damage from the Four Corners Power Plant, Fruitland, New Mexico,* Bull. 618 (Las Cruces, New Mexico State University Agriculture Experiment Station).

Randall, Alan, Berry Ives, and Clyde Eastman. 1974. "Bidding Games for Evaluation of Aesthetic Environmental Improvement," *Journal of Environmental Economics and Management* vol. 1, no. 2 (August) pp. 132–149.

Rowe, Robert D., Ralph d'Arge, and David Brookshire. 1980. "An Experiment on the Economic Value of Visibility," *Journal of Environmental Economics and Management* vol. 7, no. 1 (March) pp. 1–19.

Rowe, Robert D., and Lauraine G. Chestnut. 1982. *The Value of Visibility: Economic Theory and Applications for Air Pollution Control* (Cambridge, Mass., ABT Books).

Trijonis, J., and K. Yuan. 1978. "Visibility in the Northeast" (Research Triangle Park, N.C., U.S. Environmental Protection Agency, Office of Research and Development, Environmental Sciences Research Laboratory).

Trijonis, J., and K. Yuan. 1978. "Visibility in the Southwest: An Exploration of the Historical Data Base" (Research Triangle Park, N.C., U.S. Environmental Protection Agency, Office of Research and Development, Environmental Sciences Research Laboratory).

Outdoor Recreation

Battelle Memorial Institute. 1975. "Assessment of the Economic and Social Implications of Water Quality Improvements on Public Swimming" (Columbus, Ohio).

Bishop, Richard C., and Thomas A. Heberlein. 1980. "Simulated Markets, Hypothetical Markets, and Travel Cost Analysis: Alternative Methods of Estimating Outdoor Recreation Demand," *Wisconsin Agriculture Experimental Station Bulletin* no. 187.

Burt, Oscar R., and Durwood Brewer. 1971. "Estimation of Net

Social Benefits from Outdoor Recreation," *Econometrica* vol. 39, no. 5 (September) pp. 813–827.

Cicchetti, Charles J. 1973. *Forecasting Recreation in the United States* (Lexington, Mass., Lexington Books).

Cicchetti, Charles J., and V. Kerry Smith. 1976. *The Costs of Congestion: An Econometric Analysis of Wilderness Recreation* (Cambridge, Mass., Ballinger).

Clawson, Marion. 1959. "Methods of Measuring Demand for and Value of Outdoor Recreation," Resources for the Future Reprint No. 10 (Washington, D.C., Resources for the Future).

Clawson, Marion, and Carlton S. Van Doren, eds. 1984. *Statistics on Outdoor Recreation, Part I, The Record Through 1956;* Part II, *The Record Since 1956* (Washington, D.C., Resources for the Future).

Desvouges, William H., V. Kerry Smith, and Matthew P. McGivney. 1983. *A Comparison of Alternative Approaches for Estimating Recreation and Related Benefits of Water Quality Improvements* (Research Triangle Park, N.C., Research Triangle Institute).

Greenley, Douglas, Richard G. Walsh, and Robert A. Young. 1981. "Option Value: Empirical Evidence from a Case Study of Recreation and Water Quality," *The Quarterly Journal of Economics* vol. 96 (November) pp. 657–673.

Krutilla, John V. 1975. *The Economics of Natural Environments: Studies in the Valuation Commodity and Amenity Resources* (Baltimore, Md., Johns Hopkins University Press for Resources for the Future).

McConnell, Kenneth. 1975. "Some Problems in Estimating the Demand for Outdoor Recreation," *American Journal of Agricultural Economics* vol. 57, pp. 330–334.

Majiid, I., J. A. Sinden, and Alan Randall. 1983. "Abstract: Benefit Evaluation of Increments to Existing Systems of Public Facilities," *Land Economics* (November).

Mendelsohn, Robert, and Gardner M. Brown, Jr. 1983. "Revealed Preference Approaches to Valuing Outdoor Recreation," *Natural Resources Journal* vol. 23, no. 3 (July) pp. 607–618.

Moeller, George H., and John H. Engleken. 1972. "What Fishermen Look for in a Fishing Experience," *Journal of Wildlife Management* vol. 36, no. 4 (October).

Rankin, R. L., and J. A. Sinden. 1971. "Causal Factors in the Demand for Outdoor Recreation," *Economic Record* vol. 47 (September) pp. 418–426.

Russell, Clifford S., and William J. Vaughan. 1982. "The National Recreational Fishing Benefits of Water Pollution Control," *Journal of Environmental Economics and Management* vol. 9, no. 4 (December) pp. 328–354.

Stevens, Joe B. 1966. "Recreation Benefits from Water Pollution Control," *Water Resources Research* vol. 2, no. 2, pp. 167–182.

Sutherland, Ronald J. 1982. "A Regional Approach to Estimating Recreation Benefits of Improved Water Quality," vol. 9, no. 3 (September) pp. 229–247.

Water Pollution

Bouwes, Nicholas W., and Robert Schneider. 1979. "Procedures in Estimating Benefits of Water Quality Change," *American Journal of Agriculture Economics* vol. 61, no. 3 (August) pp. 535–539.

Council on Environmental Quality. 1981. "Contamination of Ground-water by Toxic Organic Chemicals" (Washington, D.C., CEQ).

Cronin, Francis J. 1981. "A Contingent Market Valuation of Improved Water Quality," mimeo. (Richmond, Wash., Battelle Pacific Northwest Laboratory).

Feenberg, Daniel, and Edwin S. Mills. 1980. *Measuring the Benefits of Water Pollution Abatement* (New York, Academic Press).

Greenley, Douglas A., Richard G. Walsh, and Robert A. Young, eds. 1982. *Economic Benefits of Improved Water Quality: Public Perception of Option and Preservation Values* (Boulder, Colo., Westview Press).

Hanemann, W. M. 1978. *A Methodological and Empirical Study of the Recreation Benefits from Water Quality Improvement* (Berkeley, University of California, Department of Agricultural and Resource Economics).

Unger, S. G. 1976. *National Benefits of Achieving the 1977, 1983, and 1985 Water Quality Goals,* Final Report for the U.S. Environmental Protection Agency (Washington, D.C., Development Planning and Research Associates, Inc.).

General Resource Economics

DasGupta, P. S., and G. M. Heal. 1979. *Economic Theory and Exhaustible Resources* (New York, Cambridge University Press).

Fisher, Anthony C. 1981. *Resource and Environmental Economics* (New York, Cambridge University Press).

Herfindahl, Orris C., and Allen V. Kneese. 1974. *Economic Theory of Natural Resources* (Columbus, Ohio, Charles E. Merrill).

Howe, Charles W. 1979. *Natural Resource Economics* (New York, John Wiley).

Mäler, Karl-Göran. 1974. *Environmental Economics: A Theoretical Inquiry* (Baltimore, Md., Johns Hopkins University Press for Resources for the Future).

Smith, V. Kerry, and John V. Krutilla, eds. 1982. *Explorations in Natural Resource Economics* (Washington, D.C., Resources for the Future).

Tietenberg, Thomas H. 1984. *Environmental and Natural Resource Economics: Analysis and Policy* (Glenview, Ill., Scott-Foresman).

INDEX

Note: Illustration pages are indicated by *italics*.